The
Rainbow
Sign

CHRISTIAN FUTURITY

GABRIEL FACKRE

LONDON
EPWORTH PRESS

© Gabriel Fackre 1969

First published in 1969
by Epworth Press

Printed and bound by
The Garden City Press Limited
Letchworth, Hertfordshire

SBN 7162 0077 5

To my future-oriented wife
DOROTHY
alive with 'aiglatson'

The New Reformation Series

THE past few years have seen a theological ferment which some think could herald a new Reformation. Whether it will do so is impossible to tell; in any case it is dangerous to draw historical parallels.

Yet over the last two centuries there has been a new Renaissance, a cultural revolution, which dwarfs the old. And the danger is that, in all the excitement and our desire to do something, we may be influenced more by the fashions of the age than by fidelity to truth. Christians may be tempted to count the advance of the Gospel in headlines rather than in men and women set free for living, and to substitute journalism and TV debate for the exploration of ultimate questions in the light of the new knowledge we have gained.

At the same time, theology must not be confined to the schools, and there is no more satisfactory feature of the present situation than the interchange between professionals and non-experts which paperback publishing has facilitated. After all, it is often the man or woman in the street, the office, the factory, or the laboratory who asks the questions. The attempts to answer must not be whispered in the poly-syllables of common rooms or the jargon of seminars.

It is the aim of this series to dig deep into the foundations both of Christianity and of life, but to bring what is dis-covered to the surface in a form which can be seen clearly and understood by anyone who is sensitive to the problems of our time and is willing to exercise his mind on them and on the possibility that the Christian tradition has something relevant to say. The books will not be too lengthy and they will avoid footnotes, critical apparatus and too much technicality. The authors have been chosen because they are scholars and experts in the subjects assigned to them, but also because they are alive to the contemporary world and concerned about communication.

The method will be to look for truth about the nature of the universe and of human life and personality by seeking a fruitful and illuminating interplay between modern questions and insights and traditional Christian assertions and understandings. There is no intention to seek simply a restatement of Christianity in terms 'acceptable to modern man.' The Editors believe that it is as misguided to suggest that the truth of Christianity depends on what modern man can accept as it is simply to reiterate the ancient formulations of orthodoxy. The vital questions are 'How may we be led to see what is true?'; 'What is the nature of theological truth and how is it related to other kinds?'; 'What resources have we for understanding and meeting the real needs of men?'; 'How does Christianity look in the light of our answers to these questions and how does Christianity contribute to these answers?'

We hope that this series may be a modest contribution towards *aggiornamento* if not reformation.

General Editor: GORDON S. WAKEFIELD

Advisory Board

W. RUSSELL HINDMARSH
Professor of Atomic Physics, University of Newcastle upon Tyne

DAVID JENKINS
Director of Humanum Study, World Council of Churches, Geneva. Canon Theologian of Leicester

JOHN KENT
Lecturer in Ecclesiastical History and Doctrine, University of Bristol

DAVID PATON
Hon. Canon of Canterbury

COLIN WILLIAMS
Chicago Theological Seminary

Contents

	Preface	vii
	Introduction	1
1.	Modern Hopers	16
2.	The Structure of Christian Hope	45
3.	Contemporary Conversation in Hope	70
4.	Discerning the Signs of Hope	117
	Bibliography	141
	Notes	145
	Index	151

Acknowledgements

The author and publishers are grateful for permission to use copyright material from the following works: Herman Kahn and Anthony J. Weiner, *The Year 2000*, Macmillan, New York, 1967; Teilhard de Chardin, *The Phenomenon of Man*, 1965, and *Le Milieu Divin*, 1964, Collins Publishers; J. R. R. Tolkien, *The Fellowship of the Ring*, 1966, *The Return of the King*, 1966, 'The Road Goes Ever On' from *The Hobbit*, Allen and Unwin Ltd., and Houghton Mifflin Company; Martin Luther King Jr., *Chaos or Community?* © by Martin Luther King Jr., by permission of Joan Daves; Martin Luther King, *Chaos or Community?*, Hodder & Stoughton, London, 1968; Martin Luther King Jr., *Where do We Go From Here: Chaos or Community?*, Harper & Row, Publishers of New York, U.S.A.; 'Eschatology' is reprinted by permission of G. P. Putnam's Sons from *Spilt Milk* by Morris Bishop, copyright 1942 by Morris Bishop; Edith Lovejoy Pierce, 'Revolution', copyright 1968, Christian Century Foundation, reprinted by permission from the 29 May 1968 issue of *The Christian Century*.

'God gave Noah the rainbow sign . . .'

A FREEDOM SONG

To believe in God is to be
a lily in a sun shower
open wide
to all the horizons of the sky
at once

Catching wet
and wild the wind
and rain even the futures
from which they blew

JOSEPH PINTAURO
(From *To Believe in God,*
with colour by Sister Corita,
New York 1968 p. 15)

Preface

ANTICIPATING the revived interest in a theology of hope, the New Reformation Series several years ago marked out a volume for the discussion of eschatology. The recent cascade of commentary on the subject has made this inquiry an exciting one. I am grateful to the editors for the opportunity to contribute to the dialogue.

The work introduces the reader to the whys and wherefores of the new eschatological ferment, examines some of the major figures, and compares notes with secular futurists. In and through the description of trends, however, a point of view emerges. From within this perspective on the future, alternative understandings are assessed and an attempt made to discern the contemporary 'signs of hope'. But it is an open-ended view ready to stand corrected and enlarged by the conversation on the future that is just beginning within and beyond the faith community.

The things that have influenced the direction and shape

of this perspective come clear in the pages that follow – both the newer eschatological theologies and older themes inherited from World Council of Churches reflection, involvement in the 'freedom revolution' as here understood, participation in church renewal movements, a growing concern to ferret out the meaning of developments in the life sciences, a discovery of kindred spirits among modern futurists. A few occasions and people have been of particular help in crystallizing ideas. A Springfield Massachusetts Ministers Conference in 1967 bestirred the author to first put pen to paper on the question of 'hope' in Church and world. Another assist was given by the time spent at Mansfield College, where the lively running dialogue with future-researchers Carl Braaten, Robert Jenson and Paul Crow profitably broke all the anti-shop talk rules of an Oxford Senior Common Room. Another stimulant was the exchange of thought during this year overseas with the New Reformation editors themselves, David Jenkins, Colin Williams, and Gordon Wakefield. For this sabbatical opportunity I am very grateful to Lancaster Seminary and the American Association of Theological Schools.

Finally, I want to record the debt I owe to my family. As always, my wife has shared every step along the way in the exploration. And as one grows older, his children also become partners in the adventure of ideas. They too can tell you about hobbits, sing and speculate about the future, march and dream with Martin Luther King. Many of the sections of *The Rainbow Sign* have passed under their microscopes, and, I hope, have profited from their sobering memoranda. Perhaps the scrutiny of the future generation is the litmus test of commitments that claim to be future-oriented.

July 1968
Oxford   GABRIEL FACKRE

Introduction

I have no care for Systematic Theology,
But oh, the recurrent hour of bile that brings
Fainness for specialization in Eschatology
(Greek you recall, for the study of Last Things)!

Come, day when the wealth of the world is less than tuppence,
The seas unfretted, and the monuments down,
When the proud have got their ultimate come-up-ance,
And on the seventh New York the sand lies brown:

And all my sloth and failure, all my passion
One with the sorrow of the Gaul and Goth,
And all our fireproof homes are burnt and ashen,
And in the moth-proof closets dwells the moth;

And every most unspeakable thing is spoken,
Rust in the rust-resisting pipes of brass,
And all unbreakable things at least are broken;
Shatter'd the non-shatterable glass.[1]

ESCHATOLOGY had been all bile and shattered glass to a good many in and out of the Church. But secular man has begun to write his own scenarios of the End that make the lushest imagery of *Revelation* seem pale by comparison. And something is happening too within the faith community. Eschatology has moved off the dead centre of the midnight hour to encompass the whole timepiece of the future. Tomorrow counts on that clock. And across its horizon stretches the rainbow sign.

Whirl indeed is dead and hope is queen. At least she reigns in the little land of faith where authoritative voices have proclaimed her ascendancy. Harvey Cox declares: 'Hope rather than belief may become the category through which we think as men of faith.'[2] Vernard Eller echoes the refrain in a Christian Century series on hope: 'The eschatological perspective is on the verge of becoming the great new discovery of Christian thought in our time.'[3] Or, as Charles Péguy puts it simply and forcefully, 'Hope, little hope, moves forward between her two big sisters . . . .'[4]

Is this fanfare merely the noise of a palace revolution in backwashes of modern society? Just the changing of the guard in religious country where people have grown tired of the flamboyant 'Death of God' insurrection or the flirtation with secular Christianity?

The faddism is surely there, but there is something much more significant stirring. The indication is that the borders of this kingdom stretch far beyond the 'religious' enclave. In fact, a very odd-looking alliance has given its allegiance to this new monarch. From the realm of psychiatry Karl Menniger calls for a recovery of 'hope' as an ingredient in human wholeness.[5] A new research enterprise makes the scene, 'futurology', grounded in the conviction that tomorrow is hopeful enough to speculate about its 'alternate worlds' in order to shape them now responsibly.[6] Movements that seek to rebuild cities and nations invoke the new sacred word, 'planning', and bring to birth a priesthood of 'process' catalysts which labours on the premiss that the future can be better for the vision and its active implementation now.[7] Scientists pioneering in the creation, extension and direction of life speak in apocalyptic terms of the possibility of man 'constructing himself'.[8] Political visionaries find fresh hearing among the most sober, as dramatic change seems to offer the only way through our nuclear impasse.[9] The folk idiom, pop art, and the psychedelic setting give youth a medium to express its celebration of life and its struggle to open the future.[10] The young nation alongside a young generation surges forward to make real the hopes that the new age had generated.[11] Orthodox and not-so-orthodox Marxists state their faith in the language of eschatology and begin to compare notes with Christians about their mutual hopes.[12] And the parallel developments sometimes commingle massively to learn for each other and launch joint action.

Well, it looks like one more example of the Church being the tail-light rather than the headlight. Is Christian eschatology just the current 'in' mood, with a little religious icing? We shall address ourselves to that in the heart of our study, attempting to see how faith's hope is related to man's hopes, as the latter express themselves in four representative cases. But we should note here that Christian perspective on the future is no Johnnie-come-lately interest. Eschatology is almost two thousand years old. And some say that today's secular hopers owe a debt to religious sources. But apart from the long view, even the recent revival of eschatology cannot simply be dated from a 1965 Moltmann study or a 1966 Cox essay. The end of the world was a major preoccupation of the Church in its preparation for the 1954 Evanston Assembly whose theme was 'Christ, the Hope of

3

the World'. from that not so distant past came the major contribution of a Willingen conference, the pre-Assembly and Assembly reports, the fertile thought of such ecumenical theologians as Newbigin, Calhoun, Schlink, Niles, Minear, Visser 't Hooft, Hoekendijk, Kraemer and Harkness (whose hymn, 'Hope of the World', was adopted by the Assembly).[13] Also during the same period Cullmann and others were unfolding the salvation history theme in which eschatology bulked so large.[14] The giants were at work as well – Barth, Brunner. Tillich, Heim, the Niebuhr brothers – hardly unmindful of the Kingdom of God.[15] New Testament scholarship since Albert Schweitzer carried on a running debate among realized and futurized eschatologies, and 'already – not yet' blends. Meanwhile Bultmann and his school had baptized eschatology in the waters of existentialism. And Teilhard had been ruminating since the early decades of the century on the future of man.

But for all its more recent antecedents, there is something quite fresh in the current accent on hope. Earlier eschatology was an idea whose time had not yet come. It might have heated up the world of theological academe and the conference circuit, but it did not strike fire in grass-root church leadership, ignite movements of renewal, or provide a common language for discourse with the secular community. The drama had to find roots in history itself before it could become a fighting ideology bringing to self-consciousness those very revolutionary stirrings.

The world crossed a line in the '60s that gave substance to Christian talk of the future, and put flesh on the bones of hope. One of the ingredients of the new climate has been the emergence of a cadre of change agents with their eyes fixed on the future, into whose ranks many Christians have been swept. Their freedom revolution became the Church's cause. We shall look at one of the catalysts of new church thinking and action, Martin Luther King. While there were more than a few A.W.O.L. churchmen in the army of peaceful revolution he and others led, it cannot be doubted that the direction of Christian faith, love and hope, was deeply influenced by the surge forward. When the abstractions of eschatology and the lush imagery of apocalyptic are passed through the filter of the picket line, the bars of a jail, the fury of a white mob, or a sniper's scope, they begin to look a little different. 'Reflection in the context of involvement' is more than a clever slogan. Hope becomes a life-and-death matter.

Another contemporary current that sets eschatology in fresh perspective is the acceleration of secularization, and the Church's dawning awareness of its significance. After much grumbling and rearguard harassment the Christian community is beginning to welcome the coming of age of the world as an ally to its own message and ministry. Without bowing before the pretensions of secularism – the claim of this-worldliness to omnicompetence in establishing the boundaries of reality – faith affirms secularity: man's willingness and ability finally to manage his own destiny without cowering before fates or furies, or running to religion to solve his problems. Christian secularity is the conviction that God wants a man to be a man. It celebrates the new power and determination to cut the apron string, to launch out on his own, as a birthday party that befits the majority of man.

The excited apocalyptics of the scientist suggest a certain kinship between secularity and eschatology: 'When a TV camera can be hooked to the body of a blind man so he can see, when electric charges can move the muscles of a paraplegic, when the deaf can be given electronic resonance, and when there is the possibility of the dead being given new life by deep freeze and resuscitation, then the prophecy of the Kingdom has come true that "the blind receive their sight and the lame walk . . . the deaf hear, and the dead are raised up".' We shall explore this awesome frontier of human healing and human self-definition in our chapter on signs of hope on the horizon. Suffice it to say at this point that the 'engineering' of human life is indeed a dramatic expression of the maturity of the race, maturity in the sense of being able to seize the reins of one's own future as befits an adult. Whether this new power of self-determination will also be controlled by 'maturity' in the other sense – responsible use of that power – is another matter. But here we are concerned to trace the links with eschatology, and to endeavour to see how the new capacity and mind-set of secularization have influenced Christian hope.

Secularization affects eschatology in at least two ways:

(1) It has caused theology to re-assess the roles tradition-ally assigned to man and God in the eschatological drama. Increasingly this has meant an abandonment of the assumption uncritically held by so many for so long that what God does in the Great Future, and the lesser futures that lead into it, is somehow separable from what man does. That we have courted a docetic eschatology for so long is no doubt related to the age of helplessness and dependence which mankind is now beginning to leave behind. To affirm man's coming of age as the work of God himself gives us a new perspective on eschatology as the coming of the Kingdom by God's grace, yet through human agency. If we have fought our way to an under-standing of Christ as both God and man yet one, the Church as both the Body of Christ and a body of men with sociological underside, the sacraments as gesture of Love through earthen vessels, the Christian life as the prevenience of grace yet done by the action of the will, then we must be ready as well to examine the Christian future in the light of

the same complimentarity. The secular spurt presses us towards just such an understanding, although the formulation will have to be made with the same care, fear and trembling that has characterized the confession of other Christian mysteries.

(2) Eschatology is influenced by the 'coming of age' process in goal as well as in method, in content as well as in form. When some of the very things the Christian dream portrays as signs of the Kingdom itself are forecast by responsible voices, when science-technology makes it possible to speak of a time when there may be 'no more crying nor pain, nor death for the former things are passed away', then eschatologians will begin to speak – albeit hesitantly and cautiously – about the Kingdom that is *already* breaking in in our time and history. And those who are caught up in the revolutions for human healing will echo these earthed hopes, for they will see the firstfruits of a new creation in which wolf and lamb lie down together, swords are beaten into ploughshares, and the child plays on the asp's hole. Where healing happens, there the Future breaks in. In an age in which great visions take root, Christian eschatology cannot but be affected.

As hope-talk gains momentum, it runs the risks of other accents lifted up by the Church in other times that evoked their special response. There was a ripe moment for 'Logos', 'justification by faith', 'the Church', 'the world' to be written on the banners of the Christian community. But how easy it was for a theme properly in the foreground to succumb to megalomania. One of the worst enemies of an idea whose time has come is reductionism. When an accent that is rightly to the fore elbows off the stage other themes of belief that belong to the background chorus, but none the less are still part of the company of faith, then we are in trouble. In the rush to 'puff the future' there is already

7

evidence of inordinate claims of the importance of eschatology, and of efforts to collapse the whole Christian testimony into its categories. Not only does that skew faith perilously, but it also invites a reaction that is quick to obscure the very accents we so desperately need. And it forgets the chameleon possibilities in the plunge forward towards relevance. Captivity to current notions takes the sting out of a faith whose refusal to say in a loud voice what the times are already saying is the secret of its critical power. Our task is to illumine future-oriented times from our own eschatological perspective but to do it without violence to the full orb of Christian conviction.

A related temptation is to bend the 'in' language and concepts to fit our own propensities. Eschatology becomes the word for lonely existential encounters. Eschatology means building the Kingdom of God on earth. Eschatology is evolution. Eschatology is revolution. Hope is psychologized, sociologized, biologized. Hope has nothing to do with any of these wordly things: it's belief in life after death. And so on as we grind our favourite axe on a new whetstone.

We shall not get out of this latter kind of reductionist bind by exhortations on the importance of objectivity. Responsible reading of the Christian Story comes by intimacy with its Storybook, by a deep participative life within the community of its Storytellers, and feet moving firmly across the terrain of Storyland. Out of this continuing conversation with the Bible, this company with the fathers and brethren, and from within worldly ferment and in ministry to it, will be born authentic perspectives on Christian futurity. The Pilgrim shares his life with wayfarers who track his footsteps across the landscape on which he moves. We struggle to go where he is to find our way through our parochial and half-told stories.

Along with the distortions so easily introduced into Christian faith by a powerful enthusiasm, there is a certain naïveté about companion movements that invites itself aboard. How easy it is for future-oriented Christians to conclude that all futurists are their allies. A little glance at history is good shock therapy for this illusion. Nazi philosophers made the future a central plank in their programme, with the German Christian movement following suit under the impetus of futurist speculations of W. Hauer. Totalitarian movements in general, of the left as well as the right, are noted for their willingness to sacrifice all, including the lives of their contemporaries, 'on the altar of the future'. And along with the more actively demonic forms of future-orientation, there is an easily adopted passivity towards the present. The telescope is so busy peering over the next mountain range that one has no time to negotiate the trails underfoot. A sister frailty is the preoccupation with the Big Plans of the future before which the little tasks of the 'now' pale into insignificance. The trouble is, the grand design for tomorrow can only be reached by the little steps done right now. Like the reformer who loves 'humanity' but despises persons, one may be in love with the Future, and be incapable of concern for the little todays and the real people who live in them.

But for all its risks, the fertile trinity, 'hope – future – promise', must be our fighting word for expectant times. And along with its pregnancy, there is a ripeness to some interpretations of it, more than to others. Hope is not served by a mosaic of equal parts of the thousand-and-one current eschatologies. Some concerns are rightly bashful and others bold. 'What happens to me when I die?' is a question that comes within the range of Christian hope. Nevertheless, it is not at the centre of the reflections that follow. Biblical probing has stretched the faith community's understandings of God's horizons beyond the incurved walls of this question, outwards towards history and the cosmos, and ahead towards a larger future. And when that community joins a generation with both whetted expectations and great anguish about its historical and cosmic tomorrows, it knows in its bones that anything less than the full range of its eschatological testimony and action is faithless. That is why we have chosen examples of modern hoping which move out into the open beyond the tunnels of subjectivity, towards a larger landscape. And it is why we have sketched the outlines of a Christian hope that shares a common border with this wider country, although one that stretches beyond it.

The more animated our inquiries into the dynamics of hope become, the more we begin to hear as well some gentle murmurings along the sidelines. Hope? Can it really be? Are you sure it's not just whistling in the dark?

> God's plan made a hopeful beginning
> But man spoiled his chances by sinning.
> We trust that the story
> Will end in God's glory
> But, at present, the other side's winning.[16]

And there are more strident voices. 'Ha! What is all this talk of hope! Are you blind? It is not the "hope of the world" but the "horror of the world" that meets us when we open our eyes in the morning, and shatters our dreams at night. The innocent are slaughtered by napalm; black and white, rich and poor, prepare for Armageddon; the cities burn, the sniper guns down the king of peace, apathy reigns in high places and hate rules the streets. And for those who have eyes to see behind the grim surface events to deeper things, there opens up the abyss of inner meaninglessness, the evil heart, despair, and death. Whether you look out or in, the public square or the soul, the picture is the same. Hope is as dead as God.'

So we have been told by the literature of the graveyard, by the existentialist vision of an entombed future. And the report comes as well from sober men who have felt the pain of grinding social machinery. For those who pen the dramas of our time, and many who live them, there is a 'no exit' sign up over the door of hope.

It is indeed true that the events of recent decades and those who seek to penetrate below their level, have made it impossible to dream undisturbed about a bright tomorrow. There is a deep and gnawing misery everywhere, without and within. And history is no moving staircase that will escalate us automatically out of it. The optimism of other eras is no longer a possibility for us. Two kinds in particular are ruled out: the cheerful disbelief 'that things are really not that bad' and the projection of that diagnosis into the future; or the kind of pseudo-realism that may assess the present as a disaster, but confidently anticipates better days ahead. But to know the evil that now tears away at the soft underbelly of the world, and to know as well its intransigence, is to say 'goodbye' to the naïvetés that buoyed more sanguine times.

But hope also travels without these companions. It is as fully aware of the horror of the world as the bitterest cynicism. That is one of the qualities that distinguishes today's from yesterday's hopers. We shall seek to trace this sensitivity in the new future-oriented breed, secular and Christian. They know the evil of which men are capable; they know the shadow it casts over the future. Yet they hope, and in doing so they come to learn something of 'the faith of Abraham' who 'In hope . . . believed against hope' (Rom. 4 : 18).

And because they know something of this faith, they act.

Despair immobilizes. Or else it generates erratic action that leads nowhere. Hope mobilizes. It puts together a disciplined surge towards the crack in the door of the future. And the remarkable thing is that time and again the door yields to a determined push. Hope springs locks as surely as 'hopeless case' fulfils its own prophecies.

But we are not talking about psychological tricks. Hope is as different from wishful thinking as it is from despair. There's got to be more to go on than a pragmatism that endorses future-affirming because it works. Sooner or later such hoping founders on reality, And a deeper despair is the issue. Hope starves without the food of reality. The point is, it knows where to look for that bread. And it is not so mesmerized by the abyss that it cannot find the tiny crumbs of nourishment that keep it going. They are there for the eyes of faith.

These qualities are a few of the components of a Christian futurity that is probed on the pages that follow. In fact, we shall try to make out the outlines of a design of Christian hope made up of these and other elements, in Chapter 2. And after a conversation with other eschatological visions current in Christian community in Chapter 3, we shall go on in the concluding sections to explore some signs of hope in Church and world. If we are right about our perspective and our signs, there is a gift which faith has to bring to a world transfixed by its own ugliness and powerless to act in the face of it. While an uncritical optimism is not viable, and despair helps to fulfil its own forecasts by inaction and frenzy, all that is left is hope. Can we give stones when men ask for bread?

But we cannot let ourselves get carried away with our rhetoric. We make a case here for a mission in pioneering by the Church, a sortie with the medicine of promise. But when all is said and done, the Church does not have a monopoly on this resource, nor the only mandate to share it. There are secular hopes and secular hopers. They too know something about evil, an open future, and evidence of it now on which to build towards it. We shall look early at four examples of this genre. While it may be true that biblical sources have nourished some of these modern dreams, we do not wish to make a case for it, and believe, with the most passionate of the critics of Christian hope, that our own convictions are not finally necessary to buttress men's hoping. To believe in a world come of age means that man's problems – including that one of taking the future into his own hands – are man's portion. If God wills the adulthood of the race, he wills within that goal that man should find a way to hope without dependence on resources outside himself. And that means in this case, without our deepest convictions about the God of hope himself. Until this man-sized hoping beats in the breast of 20th-century humans, faith has the servanthood task of encouraging it with whatever resources it has, including the eschatological notes in its own message and life. It also means underscoring the authentic in the human hopes which it finds on its pilgrimage towards the future. And it means, as well, the readiness to relinquish its pioneering role when men can see far enough up ahead by themselves. The pioneering-relinquishing style has characterized the social service and social action mission of the Church. It continues in a time of secularization in the ideological arena as well.

'So you are throwing in the towel after all. Christian hope is as dead as the Christian God. Both can be put out of business by an advancing secularization. If man can finally do his own tasks, if your hope and your God are really not needed in the end, what's the point of all the Christian hope-talk? It has no more meaning, any more than Christian God-talk.'

The technician mentality has such a grip on our modern psyche that nothing can get by our guards without answering the password, 'Does it work?' But are there not dimensions of reality where such a question is the wrong one? Authentic human love does not pour itself out on these conditions. It pledges itself in sickness as well as health, sorrow as well as joy, when things work as well as when they don't. So it is with the unconditional Love which reaches towards sinner as well as saint. While men can never duplicate the divine spontaneity, they are called to aspire towards it – to love God even when there is no 'payoff', no gaps to fill, to love him simply because he is there to be loved. For those who have a small inkling of what it means to love God for his own sake, there is no hand-wringing about secularization. In fact, to 'put God out of business' is a step towards the freedom of men for God. When they no more feel compelled to rush to him as a tool to bail them out, as an 'it' to be used, perhaps they will come to see that there is also there a 'thou' to be known and loved.

To put the secular function of Christian hoping out of business is not to dismantle Christian hope. There is another dimension of the future with which such orientation ahead has to do – not only the coming of a better tomorrow, but the coming of God. To believe that he is the 'One who comes' does not take away a jot or tittle of human hoping and working for the future. In fact, the burden of our story is that it undergirds them. But, for all that, it is an 'overbelief' that adds nothing to the human pilgrimage which man cannot generate from within his own resources. That is the humiliating thing about faith. It is marginal, superfluous, 'of no account'. But God will not let us forget that it is the weak things of the world and the despised that he has chosen. And he became one of them. As despised and forsaken, Christ had no case he could make for those looking for a religion that 'worked'. All he could offer was a journey on which there would be no place to lay one's head, and at the end a cross. Only the leap of hope is agile enough to find its way into that march of humiliation. But that is the kind of wayfaring a Pilgrim asks from his companions. Christian hoping is the movement ahead to be where he is, and the struggle to discover in action what it means to pray, 'Come, Lord Jesus.'[17]

1. Modern Hopers

WE BEGIN our exploration of Christian eschatology by some test bores on terrain tilted towards the future. Who are the modern hopers? We choose here four representative movements and events.

Why bother striking up a conversation with 'secular' eschatologists? One reason is that it is important to know who our friends are, and, surely, who our relatives. If there are some who talk our language, who dream the same dreams, and with whom we find ourselves marching towards common goals, then we'd better take the time to listen to them.

Listening includes learning. It would not be the first time in the history of the Church that its own perspective was illumined by currents generated outside its own household. Children of Abraham are still raised up from stones. We look therefore for ways in which modern hoping can shed light on Christian hope.

Encounter with the future-oriented does not stop with listening and learning. It is two-way traffic that involves response and sharing too. We work at understanding our neighbours-in-hope with a view to speaking our own piece, comparing notes, flinging in the air commitments to dimensions of the future which might still be closed to our fellow-pilgrims. We do not engage directly here in yes-and-no dialogue of this sort, although it is surely implicit in the following chapter that attempts to compare the design of the Christian promise with the structure of contemporary hopes. In this short study it is enough to try to introduce the participants to each other and encourage a conversation that has yet to be seriously launched.

When kinship is discovered between the world's hopes and the Church's (as is most evident in our first example) there is the inevitable impulse to trace the ties to a long-lost union in which Christian seed did its fertilizing work. As there is a certain eagerness to show how secularization is the child of biblical nourishment, so someone is bound to claim that the lineage of modern hoping can be traced to Christian ancestry. That may be, but it is not part of our job here to do this kind of heraldics. In fact, overzealous claims of this sort sometimes smack of triumphalism. God is big and free enough to do his work without benefit of clergy and their tools. He may have given birth to man's maturation, and whetted expectations too, quite apart from Christian nurture. We praise him for that, and leave it to historians with no agenda to show otherwise. Our job is to find out what he is up to now, to discern the signs of these times and those towards which we move. Let us be about that business.

I have a Dream

As these words are written, the world watches the last rites of Martin Luther King. And many, whose reddened eyes follow the journey of the wagon hearse across their television screen, despair. What is the future of the cause of love and justice for which he gave his life? Are the explosions in the ghettoes and the hate-filled response of white gun-hoarders signs of things to come?

In his own lifetime King faced tragedies and setbacks of similar magnitude. While others ran for cover, or spun out philosophies of defeat or desperation, he maintained his 'stride towards freedom', the vision he had fixed upon. He was one of the great hopers of our time. We can learn something about coming to terms with our own horror at what has happened, and what it seems to bode, by listening to him, especially as he confronted the gathering storms of recent years. Although it is not our principal concern at this point, perhaps we can learn as well about the springs of Christian hope itself.

King's soul was seared by the wounds of his people. Moreover he had no illusions about the white man's readiness to put aside their blunt and/or subtle instruments of torture:

The central quality in the Negro's life is pain—pain so old and so deep that it shows in almost every moment of his existence. . . . Being a Negro in America . . . means being a part of the company of the bruised, the battered, the scarred and the defeated. Being a Negro in America means trying to smile when you want to cry. It means trying to hold on to physical life amid psychological death. It means the pain of watching your children grow up with clouds of inferiority in their mental skies. It means having your legs cut off, and then being condemned for being a cripple. It means seeing your mother and father spiritually murdered by the slings and arrows of daily exploitation, and then being hated for being an orphan. Being a Negro in America means listening to suburban politicans talk eloquently against open housing while arguing in the same breath that they are not racists. It means being harried by day and haunted by night by a nagging sense of nobodyness and constantly fighting to be saved from the poison of bitterness. It means the ache and anguish of living in so many situations where hopes unborn have died.[1]

King's agony over the ruthless smashing of black bodies and souls, from the stench and death of the slave ships to the bombs of southern rednecks and the duplicity of Northern politicians, was compounded in recent years by the wave of desperation that swept through the ranks of his own fellow freedom fighters. It was sharply driven home when he experienced his first public booing among allies, and then saw the fighting word, 'black power', emerge on the Mississippi march of 1966. While questioning the ambiguity of the slogan (he notes that it could mean anything from aggressive violence through defensive violence to education in black identity and the struggle for political power), he was committed to many of its accents: the assertion that Afro-Americans should lead their own revolution, exercise control over their own community matters, develop black political, economic and social power, and affirm the dignity of their colour and heritage which for so long has been eviscerated by stereotype, distortion and silence. Of course his non-violent philosophical commitments were set against the overtones of extreme interpretations. But also his reasoning was pragmatic, for he felt that any proposals to encourage black separatism or aggressive violence were an invitation to black self-destruction in a society that was 90 per cent white and in control of massive resources of reprisal. On this basis alone, black aggression could only be seen as a counsel of despair, 'black suicide', born from a loss of hope.

A fundamental factor in King's refusal to be sucked under by the massiveness of the evil or the new despair was a force that wrenched his gaze away from the present abyss and in another direction: the future. With uncanny premonition of his own fate, yet pointing beyond it to the vision that controlled his whole life, he told Memphis fighters for trashman justice:

> I don't know what will happen to me . . . we've got some difficult days ahead, but it doesn't matter to me now. . . . I've been to the mountain top. . . . Like anybody I'd like to live a long life. . . . But I'm not concerned about that now. I just want to do God's will. And he's allowed me to go up the mountain. And I've looked over, and I've seen the Promised Land. I may not get there with you, but I want you to know tonight that we as a people will get to the Promised Land. So I'm happy tonight. I'm not fearing any man. Mine eyes have seen the glory of the coming of the Lord![2]

In these biblical cadences which in a few short days became the treasures of the Freedom Movement, King disclosed the power that kept him going. It was a vision without which he believed his people would perish. It was a picture of a future out of which God was coming with his victory. Whereas the timid and the devious have time and again turned this biblical dream of a knit-together world into 'pie in the sky when you die', King threw it on the screen of tomorrow in the hard shapes and lustrous colours of this world. For the haulers of garbage there would be justice and freedom now. That hope for history itself was nowhere more memorably unfurled for both black and white than from the steps of the Lincoln Memorial on the Washington March of 1963:

> I have a dream that one day this nation will rise up and live out the true meaning of its creed . . . that all men are created equal. I have a dream that one day even the state of Mississippi, a state sweltering in the heat of oppression, will be transformed into an oasis of freedom and justice. I have a dream that my four little children will one day live in a nation where they will not be judged by the colour of their skin but by the content of their character. . . . So let freedom ring. From the prodigious hilltops of New Hampshire, let freedom ring. From the mighty mountains of New York, let freedom ring. From the heightening Alleghenies of Pennsylvania, let freedom ring. But not only that; let freedom ring from Stone Mountain of Georgia.

> Let freedom ring from every hill and molehill of Mississippi. And
> when this happens, when we let it ring, we will speed that day when
> all of God's children, black men and white men, Jews and Gentiles,
> Protestants and Catholics, will be able to join hands and sing in the
> words of the old Negro spiritual, 'Free at last, free at last, Thank God
> Almighty, we're free at last!'[3]

A secular and sceptical age may listen wistfully to the
oratory, and marvel at the enthusiasm it stirs in its converts,
but sooner or later the question will be put: Do not the
religious roots of this talk of a reconciled world betray it as
a fantasy? The dream is a pipe-dream. We will be worse for
it in the long run, for it holds out impossible hopes. When
shattered on the rock of facts, it will leave men more
desperate than ever. And the proof is the rise of a black
nationalism that is the fruit of crushed expectations.

King was not so naïve as to base his hope on religious
fantasies. Nor did he take the route of a clever, but ultimately fragile psychologizing which reasons that we ought to
give the people a shot of hope if that is what will move
them to action. The trouble with the latter is that it plays
out sooner or later when it comes up against facts that do
not bear it out. King's hope had taproots in the soil of both
fact and responsible faith. The latter led to the former on
which we now focus, the secular solidities of his expectation. His hope was grounded in the evidence that the present was open to the future. To resist that datum is to pay
the price, as did Sheriff Clark who 'stumbled against the
future'.[4] King had little use for those who wallowed in orgies
of self-congratulation about 'how far the Negroes had
come'. But he resisted as well the sour-mouth dismissal of
the years of struggle. While mincing no words about the
continuing, and in some respects worsening, dehumanization of black brothers, he refused to deride the advances. He
viewed the black man's surge towards unified action to gain

legislative and social advances as the signs of seizing his humanity from the white oppressor:

He gained manhood in a nation that had always called him 'boy'.[5]

Hope was no pious fiction because the signs of its inbreaking could already be discerned:

These were the values he won that enlivened hope even while sluggish progress made no substantial changes in the quality or quantity of his daily bread.[6]

The confidence he had in the power of his *modus operandi* – the march, boycott, selective buying, sit-in, and as a last recourse a civil disobedience that accepts the consequences of its act, done in militant but non-violent idiom – was not only born from the vision of reconciliation, but also from the hard evidence of history that the method worked. He sought to steer between the Scylla of hate and violence and the Charybdis of passive persuasion, and found in Mahatma Ghandi an example of a fusion of love and hope that mounted a successful revolution. And he pointed to the victories at Montgomery, Birmingham, Washington, and Selma, and signs of opening in northern cities as portents of what peaceful thrust towards change could do.

A vital bit of evidence to which he returned time and again to win credence for the future's promise was the work that black and white had done together in the Movement. That this shared commitment could happen was proof that it could again be so, and ultimately so.

Every time a Negro in the slums of Chicago or on the plantations of Mississippi sees Negroes and whites honestly working together for a common goal, he sees new grounds for hope.[7]

Or, as he puts it poignantly in the dedication of his last book written in the uprush of tendencies towards black separatism:

22

To the committed supporters of the civil rights movement, Negro and white, whose steadfastness amid confusions and setbacks gives assurance that brotherhood will be the condition of man, not the dream of man.[8]

Running like a red thread through the signs that are data for hoping is a common theme: the evidence is all of a special kind. The proof that expectations can materialize is the hard fact that men right now can do something to affect their future. The evidence is not that the fates or furies have been kind, and therefore the black community can relax on an escalator upward. Rather the situation is that no one controls tomorrow, particularly not the white overlords who for so long cultivated the myth that their power could not be challenged. The non-violent uprising had shown that the future could be bent towards the black man as well as away from him. What it took was the seizure of initiative:

when slaves unite, the Red Seas of history open . . .[9]

While Martin Luther King was not sure he could reach the Promised Land with his people, he was determined to show them that the enemy was not invulnerable and the waters could part.

Out of this network of commitments, insights, and hopes a radical mandate took form. King's life was one long call to arms. In the grip of a Future that belongs to his Lord and scattered its seeds in the present, he became the voice of the voiceless. He sought to call the Nebuchadnezzars to account and shamed the conscience of white society. But he fully realized that vested interest is not moved by exhortation and appeals to conscience. The real changes would come about only when the black dispossessed put futility behind and manned the non-violent barricades.

. . . the Negro cannot achieve emancipation by passively waiting for the white race voluntarily to grant it to him. The Negro has not gained a single right in America without persistent pressure and agitation.[10]

This urgency was no rhetoric or frenzied mobilization for *ad hoc* encounters. It was, increasingly, a carefully planned review of how breakthroughs could be accomplished, a strategy which required 'studying the levers of power'.[11] Call to action meant selecting the right issue at the right time, the cultivation of selective coalitions, the exploration of the union movement – or a section of it – as a vehicle for work. In short King believed that the future was hopeful because men could control their destiny if they massed all their skill and dedication for a united assault upon it. Such a conviction was born of deep religious faith, but faith which believed that the God of the future gave man the key to unlock the future – if he chose. Towards that future he lived, and for it he died.

The Year 2000

From the Delphic oracle to the prognoses of Wells and Huxley, the seer has exercised a fascination for man. Sometimes forecasting becomes a major social or literary preoccupation, as it did forty years ago, when a rash of books was published attempting to pull aside the veil of tomorrow: Haldane's *Daedalus, or Science and the Future*, McNair Wilson's *Pygmalion, or the Doctor of the Future*, Dobrée's *Timotheus, or The Future of the Theatre*, etc. The future again moved into view in the mid-'60s.

There are some important differences between the new futurists and the old prophets, as Daniel Bell, the chairman of the Commission on the Year 2000, observes in his comparison of the two. In his introduction to Herman Kahn and Anthony J. Weiner's *The Year 2000*, Bell characterizes the modern effort in futurology as a more serious venture than the impressionistic, half-jocular, and highly individualistic forecasting of the '20s. Today, futurism makes use of the best available statistical techniques, computer data, and methods of social analysis. While it does not discount the imaginative, and in fact draws upon the prognostications of both the artist and 'macro-historian' (Toynbee, Berdyaev, Sorokin) and does some bold speculating of its own, it is carried out within the framework of 'growing sophistication about methodology and an effort to define the boundaries – intersections and interactions – of social systems that come into contact with each other'.[12] Contemporary futurology is the effort to chart the forward dynamics of modern history on the basis of the careful sifting and extrapolation of solid data. And it is done as a team venture in cross-disciplinary inquiry which further distinguishes it from the solo performance of the classic seer.

Another difference Bell notes is the goal of the modern futurist. Their efforts are bent towards influencing social policy. Convinced that men still have time to use accelerating technology for responsible ends, and aware of the vastness of the changes necessitated (e.g. the 'rebuilding of American cities', the 'expansion of medical services'), futurists believe that it is necessary to stir centres of social power to anticipatory action and planning. It is not unusual for the fast-developing centres of research on the future to be in conversation with governments and other corporate decision-makers. The risk entailed in these affiliations, especially as they touch on military prognosis, have brought the 'think-tanks' under the kind of critical exposure of a Report from Iron Mountain.

Implicit in Bell's description of futurology is another factor that takes on prominence as Kahn and Weiner expound some of the highlights of their research to date at the Hudson Institute. The urgency about probing the future is directly related to the horrendous possibilities that lie ahead. The capabilities for thought-control that range from refined devices of universal surveillance to manipulation of brain

25

processes through electrode implant, drug, atmospheric change; the risks of a world smothered by its own wastes, devastated by thermonuclear warfare touched off either by accident or because the miniaturizing of atomic weaponry makes them available to the criminal; the erasure of man literally, by 'death ray' possibilities in lasers, or more subtly by developments which blur the line of 'the human' and hence erode commitments to human dignity – these and many other options are canvassed in 'scenarios' and speculations which cannot be dismissed as science fiction for there is just enough hard data in the present to give them credibility. In a paragraph that the authors feel is sufficiently important to include twice in the text, they say:

> Technology raises issues of 'accelerated nuclear proliferation; of loss of privacy; of excessive governmental and or private power over individuals; of dangerously vulnerable, deceptive and degradable overcentralization; of decisions becoming necessary that are too large, complex, important, uncertain, or comprehensive to be left to mere mortals—whether private or public; of new capabilities that are so inherently dangerous that they are likely to be disastrously abused; of too rapid or cataclysmic change for smooth adjustment . . .'[14]

In the light of these observations it is understandable why Kahn and Weiner remark in the concluding pages of their book:

> Few of us are likely to return to the naïve optimism of the Enlightenment, to the rationalistic confidence in historical progress that is still dying slowly in both East and West.[15]

It is one thing to fling the rhetoric of Domesday from a Hyde Park soapbox and another to launch a long-range research inquiry into the shape of the most frightening prospects of tomorrow. The methodical analysis of 'the next thirty-three years' is itself a sign that the whole story has not been told about the expectations of futurology after the most dismal possibilities are reviewed. The enterprise itself and the think-tank's effort to 'lobby for the future' are signs of a belief in a wider horizon than a thermonuclear glow. In fact, the sombre scenarios, while taken with full seriousness, yet fall to a large extent into the nightmare possibilities of the 21st century, and are therefore, by the authors' reckoning, much more highly speculative than their projections into the nearer future of 'the next thirty-three years', the real arena of their studies. Moreover, the apocalyptic possibilities are largely extrapolations of some of the 'Canonical Variations' in the spectrum of 'alternative futures' within the thirty-three year spread. 'Canonical Variations' is the authors' phrase for options that stretch the mind creatively towards the future, but are less likely than the configuration they term the 'Standard World' of tomorrow. The latter, while 'improbable' because of the ease with which unforeseen variables can intrude to upset the direction is, however, *less* unlikely than the eight Canonical Variations sketched out to complete the range of options. The Standard World, which represents the consensus of a group of Hudson Institute researchers, while filled with such ominous signs as the probability of enlarged violence, posits, nevertheless, the clumsy but continuing containment of major dehumanizing upheavals. The possibility of an awkwardly controlled development of Faustian powers, or, in the more modest idiom of the futurologists, the thesis that a cataclysm is more unlikely than the unlikeliness of their Standard World, mark them as among the modern hopers. The future is not closed.

It is not wishful thinking that turns the eyes of the futurist towards an open tomorrow. In the very nature of a Standard World are the grounds for hope. By definition, a Standard World is an extrapolation based on contemporary evidence. The researchers have examined in great detail regnant technological, political, economic, social and philoso-

27

phical tendencies. Drawing these together into a construct of thirteen interacting components, they have established a 'basic, long-term multifold trend'. With origins as far back as the late middle ages, the course of this trajectory is viewed as likely to continue through the next three decades. Elements in the flow include the movement towards: 'Increasingly Sensate (empirical, this-worldly, . . . pragmatic, . . .) cultures . . . Accumulation of scientific and technological knowledge . . . Worldwide industrialization . . . Population growth . . . Urbanization . . . Literacy and education . . . Increasing universality of multifold trend'.[16]

Within this framework, the authors look at the particulars of gross national products as they are now and how they might continue, technological innovation, ideological currents, etc., in the light of present performance, pace of change, and direction. The Canonical Variations are also examined with their real but less likely projections. In both cases, extensions are made in 'surprise-free' terms (or relatively surprise-free in the case of the Canonical Variations), that is to say, on the assumption that the momentum of the present gives basic clues to the future. Full recognition, however, is also given to surprises that might shatter the Standard World expectations, and some effort made to explore what these might be and how they might affect the course of history. In any case, Kahn and Weiner do try to root their projections in the solidities of the past and present, as these are combed through by social methodologies.

There is another contemporary factor that shapes the researcher's future-orientation. Perhaps it marks him as a man of his time, in so far as it is an expression of some of the components in the multifold trend such as the Sensate, democratic, innovative factors. He believes that the future can be affected by choices that are now made. While the

28

past's pressure constricts the range of choices that can be made, it has not as yet so tightened around tomorrow that man cannot by his own ingenuity and action alter its course. 'If man may never be completely in control of his fate, perhaps at least he may rise to partial control.'[17] Whether the predisposing factors are threatening or promising, it is still man's portion to tip the scale.

Out of this conviction, that the future is still open enough for men to influence it, comes the mandate to work unsparingly at the task. Bell sees the significance of the discipline of futurology in just this effort:

In his famous distinction between *fortuna* and *virtù* (in Chapter 25 of *The Prince*) Machiavelli argued that half of men's actions are ruled by chance, and the other half are governed by men themselves. This volume, and the work of the Commission on the Year 2000, is an effort to change that balance.[18]

The authors themselves view their task in essentially moral terms. Noting that such talk comes hard to many in research circles they urge a step beyond intellectual aloofness:

It is a curious comment on our current milieu that the invocation of the language of morality is almost completely restricted to the intellectually unrespectable extreme right or left. No doubt this is because abuse of moralistic exhortation has made it embarrassing to the more sophisticated; yet it may be this very characteristic of our times that make plausible some of the possibilities we raised [the 'nightmares']¹[19]

The mission of the futurologist, therefore, is to add his support to the possibility of realizing a world relatively free of the nightmares. In terms of the category of choice, he is seeking to keep alive and widen the indeterminacy he experiences in the present. Because of the rapidity of change and the increasing difficulty of using inherited formulas, he sees as a fundamental challenge the securing of the freedom of generations unborn:

> Above all, there must be a concern for perpetuating those institutions that protect freedom of human choice—not only for today's individuals and the pluralistic social groups that would want their views represented, but more important, for those who will follow us—those who in the future may experience their problems differently and would not want to find that we have already—unnecessarily and unwisely—foreclosed their choices and altered their natural and social world irretrievably.[20]

There is a promissory moral passion in the most sensitive of the modern futurists. But it is joined to a modesty in method and anticipation appropriate for an enterprise striving for the credential of a 'new science'. Thus futurology, hopeful enough about the next decades to invest time and labour in tracing out their contours, sees its work as 'heuristic' and 'praepedeutic'. In his sketching of alternative futures from trended data, the new futurist seeks to be a catalyst of the kind of thought about tomorrow, and action towards it, that will make it fit for human habitation.

Frodo Lives

Commenting on the mood of modern literature and painting Tillich said just before he died:

> Art in all its forms can show three states of mind: hopelessness, foolish hope, and genuine hope. If we look at our present artistic creations we find that artistic expressions of hopelessness by far prevail. . . . Artistic interpretations of genuine hope . . . are rare today.[21]

For a long time we have assumed that art is the most sensitive barometer of the winds of an era. If Tillich is right in his diagnosis, either today's new wave of hope is illusory, or the art community has not yet caught up with contemporary reality. Or it may well be that the artistic weathervane must be sought on odder-looking barns where the conventional wisdom does not hold sway. There would be a nice bit of artistic irony if the best art of an era were born in the unlikeliest of places – let us say in some philologist's library instead of a Left Bank café – and had to do with the unlikeliest of material – let us say elves and Ents rather than ids and angst.

And indeed we here nominate Oxford don, J. R. R. Tolkien, with his Hobbit world, as a literary candidate for the cadre of modern hopers. But we have to be very careful about how we do it. The material itself and its rationale cannot be approached in the same way as the message-oriented art of our day. That fact itself says something about its meaning.

Frodo's journey to Mordor to dispose of the Ring has been interpreted by knowing cryptographers to mean everything from harnessing the H-bomb to a plot to divert the proletariat into fantasy land and away from the struggle to overthrow their capitalist oppressors.[22] Tolkien's retort has been:

> As for any inner meaning or 'message', it has in the intention of the author none. It is neither allegorical nor topical. . . . I cordially dislike allegory in all its manifestations, and always have done so since I grew old and wary enough to detect its presence. I much prefer history, true or feigned, with its varied applicability to the thought and experience of readers. I think that many confuse 'applicability' with 'allegory'; but the one resides in the freedom of the reader, and the other in the purposed domination of the author.[23]

We therefore must disavow the attempt to impose upon the story our agenda, including that of finding here some clarion call to hope by the author. But Tolkien's remarks about 'applicability' are part of the picture too. And undergirding that is a commitment to the 'freedom of the

31

reader'. What good is this freedom if it is not seized and stewarded? One strong argument for exercising the freedom to trace out application of this work is its startling reception, particularly among youth and young adults. Tolkien himself wonders about the response it has triggered and the cultic activity it has evoked. Some sort of chord in the modern psyche has been struck. Let us use the freedom of the reader to locate it.

Taking issue with a reviewer who called the *Lord of the Rings* a 'jolly' story, Tolkien pointed out that there is an intense sense of evil that pervades the book. Citing Simone de Beauvoir's observation that finitude exercises a fascination for people, he went on to say that death is a 'keyspring' in his tale.[24] In addition to the regular harassment, setbacks and losses of the companions who carry the Ring to its destination, there is an air of futility that hangs over the journey itself. Treebeard, the forest ally, reflects the spirit of the pilgrimage when he says to Pippin and Merry: 'Of course, it is likely enough that we are going to *our* doom: the last march of the Ents.'[25] And at one of the many ebbtides in the pilgrimage Sam Gamgee meditates:

> But the bitter truth came home to him at last: at best their provision would take them to their goal; and when the task was done, there they would come to an end, alone, houseless, foodless in the midst of a terrible desert. There could be no return.[26]

Without attributing the dour notes to the war through which England was passing when many of the hobbit tales were written, it is surely possible to say that the power of evil is given its full due. And a generation that lives under the same Damoclean sword will not find it hard to discover parallels in its own experience, especially for those whose future stretches before them, yet is rendered so tenuous by the threat of world conflict or other social disasters.

But in spite of the odds that seem stacked against the

pilgrims, there is a drawing power to the future. The travellers' song, now put to music and translated in elfish language in a separate volume, says it this way:

> The Road goes ever on and on
> Down from the door where it began
> Now far ahead the Road has gone,
> And I must follow if I can.[27]

Frodo is mesmerized by the point out ahead, his hobbit companions constantly discuss it, Gandalf the wizard strives to penetrate it, and all move towards it irrevocably. As it is the future that makes the world interesting, according to Teilhard de Chardin, so it is the goal and the path to it that gives this story its life. Tolkien chose the framework of a journey with an object because it is a form that enabled him to carry out the long narrative project he had set for himself. In doing it, he settled his characters into a posture befitting a future-oriented generation. The road that stretches out ahead is an accurate symbol for such a time.

But what does in fact lie up ahead? That is the question. Doom, maybe, even probably. But not for sure. There is a faint glimmer of possibility in the future.

> The Road goes ever on and on . . .
> Pursuing it with weary feet
> Until it joins some larger way,
> Where many paths and errands meet.
> And whither then? I cannot say.[28]

The door of tomorrow is not slammed in the face of the pilgrim. The future is still open. Sam in the middle of the aforementioned despair draws on wells not easily drained.

> But even as hope died in Sam, or seemed to die, it was turned to a new strength. Sam's plain hobbit-face grew stern, almost grim as the will hardened in him, and he felt through all his limbs a thrill, as if he was turning into some creature of stone and steel that neither despair nor weariness nor endless barren miles could subdue.[29]

33

Treebeard, almost sure of disaster, can also go on to finish the speech cited earlier:

> But if we stayed at home and did nothing, doom would find us anyway, sooner or later. That thought has long been growing in our hearts; and that is why we are marching now. . . . Now at least the last march of the Ents may be worth a song. Aye, . . . we may help the other peoples before we pass away.[30]

And in fact they did. Held by a slender thread, 'hope' nevertheless swings its way through the tale. It is surprising how often the word itself occurs and how frequently the subject is discussed by the companions. Legolas the elf sounds a recurring refrain shouted at the future in the teeth of its uncertainty: 'Yet do not cast all hope away. Tomorrow is unknown. Rede oft is found at the rising of the sun.'[31] And Aragorn echoes it as he finds remnants of Merry's and Pippin's belongings at the scene of a battle: 'I will take these things, hoping against hope, to give them back.'[32] Thus an uncertain end allowed at least for the possibility of a good one, however slim.

Is this not a vain hope finally when all the cards are stacked against you? But is all the evidence that of a 'No' written across the future? The factor which rescues the future from futility – and keeps the story wound up as well – is the trailmakers of hope. Things happen that seem to show that the mission can be carried out. 'Frodo lives', as the youth culture button puts it. The most striking thing of all is that the puny resources of a ragged company of the tiny and tired do make headway. From the simple gardener, Sam Gamgee, through the childlike Merry and Pippin, to the unlikely hobbit Frodo and the aged Gandalf of fading wizardry, a force is mustered for a journey against the awesome armies of Mordor, and stumbles ahead with resiliency and resurrecting power. By an odd concatenation of events it even accomplishes its mission. But the point we make here is that there always seem to be some hints of hope that push them on. It is not daydreaming, not hope in hope, but hope earthed, however tiny the specks of it. And at the centre of this evidence is the strange power of the powerless to affect their future.

The pull of the future, fortified by signs of its inbreaking, combines to call the band of pilgrims forward. Aware of the traps and racked by the possibility of defeat, promise nevertheless evokes act:

> . . . I must follow if I can

or in the words of another pilgrim song:

> Home is behind, the world ahead,
> And there are many paths to tread
> Through shadows to the edge of night,
> Until the stars are all alight.[33]

Tolkien has written a work to which a pilgrim generation resonates. To the forward focus of characters and content must be added as well a *modus operandi* which in its own way expresses the same open-ended quality. The effort to remove the heavy hand of author manipulation frees the reader from closure towards fresh meanings that could not be anticipated by the writer. The literature of despair habitually uses its material to control the reader, and thus embodies its messages in its medium. Hopelessness is conveyed by slamming shut all doors but the option of nothingness. A central quality of hope is the evidence that the future is open and that man can influence it. Writing which honours that openness and the role of the reader as a participant in shaping the yet-to-be-decided outcome takes its place in the ranks of today's future-oriented. By that standard, as well as by the particulars of its application, hobbitry is a hopeful art.

After Treblinka

We conclude our catalogue of modern hopers with the most unlikely of all evidence: The crime against humanity that was Treblinka. In a documented story of the experimental extermination camp in which 800,000 innocents were slaughtered, Jean-Francois Steiner has cut through misery and myth to uncover the heart of a hope that beat strongly enough to generate revolt.[34] In the midst of so hideous an evil that the tough-minded reviewer confesses to putting it down in order to get second wind, one thousand Jews determined not to be sheep led to a slaughter. They did because they saw a 'light at the end of the tunnel'. It had to be a very special hope that could survive the monstrous evidence of hopelessness – literally – on every side in lines of naked and unsuspecting women and children preparing for their 'baths', and the piles of charred bodies in 'Camp No. 2' which they themselves, as the workhorses of the Nazis, were readying for the final inferno. It was a hope born of shattered hopes. Let us see first what had to go before something new could come.

Steiner believes that the Nazis were able to proceed unimpeded by the Jewish community, in their genocide for so long, because of their skilful exploitation of a deep-going commitment of the Covenant people to life itself. 'An ancestral urge' and a duty associated with their election for special mission, this unquenchable urge to live provided grist for the mill of the 'technicians'. Those charged with carrying out the mass murder discovered that if they kept open a small 'margin of hope', if the station to the camp of no return was pleasantly decorated for arriving trainloads, if assurances were given with bars of soap that only a shower awaited, docility was probable.

Favouring them in this psychological manipulation was

the fact that even Jews whose memory included the history of European pogroms could not conceive of some line of Judaism not surviving. Nor could they imagine that mitigation of the torment would not be possible if a passive stance was taken. Mated to that was the long-standing 'loser' role of the Jew in Gentile society in which the 'goy' always seemed to be on top, and there was no possibility foreseeable in which the Jew could challenge this perennial 'winner', secure in his superior resources of tyranny.

Religion too served the purposes of accommodation in a variety of ways. For some it provided an explanation of the massiveness of suffering: God was punishing the Jews for their sins, or issuing a warning and call to penitence. For others it provided a ritual escape from the horror of the present, an unceasing dialogue with God, reeling back and forth from ecstasy to anger, an eternal 'Now' which took the sting out of the historical 'now'. For others it meant that God would vindicate his electing love and somehow rescue his chosen people from their misery. And for still others it meant, in the long-standing framework of traditional otherworldliness, an assurance that all the wrong would be righted in the world to come – so why fight the passing evil immediacies? For them the brutal Nazi humour that called the walk to the gas chamber 'the road to heaven' was true.

As long as all these hopes twitched with the slightest life, true hope was dead. 'They had not yet touched the bottom; therefore they could not yet begin to rise again.'[35] How did resurrection come for a small company at Treblinka, and what was its shape?

One by one the illusions were exposed for what they were, a 'comedy of hope'. A few began to see the enormity of the Nazi plan, the total extinction of the Jew, even of the memory of the existence of his race. Such an enterprise meant, first, that the future of the Covenant nation was itself in question. Not only did the Nazis intend that goal, but the coldblooded 'success' of the technicians' methods seemed to render it a possibility. And second, it meant, quite personally, that one's own meagre chance to survive even the worst holocaust was now extinguished. The Nazis meant to wipe out Judaism and they were capable of achieving it.

When that realization dawned, anodynes were exposed for what they were. The religious scaffolding tumbled with the superstructure. The more ineluctable the end seemed, the less persuasive became the talk of miraculous rescue. The more massive the horror, the more difficult it was to believe that it somehow fitted into an inscrutable divine plan. The more the goy security was compared with their own insecurity, the more the theory of suffering became untenable.

But the ending of vain hopes was not enough to turn the tide. It could well thrust men into deeper despair. So many a Jewish leader believed who tried to keep the worst of Nazi design from his people, when he knew in his heart these things were true. Without another ingredient, the removal of the props of illusion would only collapse whatever spirit remained, and make the last moments living hell itself, perhaps even giving the world at large material for some of its sordid theories of Jewish cowardice.

The new constituent began to make its first halting appearance in an outbreak of suicides among the death-camp workers. What happens when a man mounts a box, belts his neck to a pipe, and a fellow slave pulls the crate away? Two things: A man has shown that he himself will decide how his life shall end. And another man has shown his solidarity with him. Together they have thwarted the technicians. It means that the slave has some control over the future. The technicians did not have so tight a grip on tomorrow that a Jew could not wrest it from him. A pyrrhic victory indeed, some will say; for it took away the very life that gave the future any meaning. Not so. For despair and inaction were bred by the conviction that the goys' hegemony over the future could not be broken. And ever so slight a shaking of that article of faith might well be the beginning of the end of tomorrow's 'No exit'. It was.

The evidence of an open future began to mount. One bit was the report coming to the camp of the resistance in the Warsaw ghetto, to the great annoyance of the oppressor. Another was a trickle of escapes from the camp. Another was a miscalculation by the camp commander of a whipping given by a 'trusty' leader of the aborning resistance to an inmate, that was in fact calculated to facilitate an escape. Another was the shooting of the camp bully by a desperate Jew, and the re-adjustment of technician procedure in the wake of it – more beguiling doses of psychological sedation, but for all that, an actual response forced on the Nazis by the action of one of their number. And yet another was the heart-rending call to revolt by the shreds of a man on public view for a misdemeanour, as he coughed and bled out his last.

What happened in these successive waves of futurity was the re-direction of the deep-going drive towards life away from passivity towards action for tomorrow. The evidence that one could make a difference joined itself to the surge, and out of this mix came the explosion of revolt. It took the form of a covenant hope. It looked for and worked for the day when the story would be told, and the world would be shocked awake by the enormity of the Nazi crimes. The first-hand report of this horror would be the only way the world could be stirred from its slumbers and halt the genocidal drift. But more, a report from a survivor that had fought his way out would also show the world,

39

and the generations to come, that the Jew was not led like a sheep to the slaughter. He had fought back. His heirs could be proud. To be a Jew was to be a man. As an organizer of the resistance put it to a prospective participant, ' "Do you think we can do something?" The answer served as his definitive test.'[36]

For those for whom religion was still an option – and strangely, even for many who had become confessing atheists – God was an ally of this hope to whom they poured out the Shema, with whom they fought and argued, and finally celebrated as the God of Israel who called them to action. He wanted them to tell the story. Now the call to penitence was not to the Jew but to the world. The burning bodies of the Jews were signal fires of warning. Wake up, you silent and sleeping! We shall wake you up by Yahweh's grace and claim.

Hope became deed when the last rows were readied for the funeral pyres. The Nazis began to suspect that desperation would breed a final act of resistance and were increasing their vigilance. One more miscalculation, for the Jews had crossed that last bridge long since. The technicians were going to have to deal with a carefully spun web, long in the making, to which they had contributed not only with guns from their own stores but from a hope they inadvertently had seeded. They were dealing with men who coolly weighed the avenues out, who had already died their own death, who were mesmerized by a goal out ahead and believed by the little controls they had exercised on the future, that it could be realized. 'Once again the Jews had become the "People with the stiff necks".'[37]

The revolt came after several heart-rending false starts and unforeseen incidents that culminated in a premature triggering off of the uprising. Under the withering fire of the guards and reinforcements, the personal death expectation of many a freedom fighter was fulfilled; but so was the hope. Six hundred escaped. Of these, forty survived the further harassment and misery of life in the forest. They are still alive today. They told their story. And told it again on the pages of *Treblinka* for an age that might have forgotten the lesson of its fathers.

After Auschwitz, a sensitive Jewish theologian could no longer find it in his heart to believe in the God of his fathers. The enormity of that evil has driven him into a hopeless faith in which God dies as surely as his people. During and after Treblinka something else happened in the souls of other Jews. No, not a simple rebirth of faith which piety can put on its scorecard in some sort of ghastly gamesmanship. We leave aside for the moment the question of faith, and look instead at hope. Here, in the abyss, some men were able to prop themselves up and look beyond the 'now' to what was yet to be – to what they believed they could make be. They threw off the shackles of the given. And because they dared to hope; they dared to act. Ironically, Simone de Beauvoir writes the introduction to *Treblinka*. While it puts the stamp of the existentialist establishment on the book, it might better have been done by some Teilhardian countryman, student revolutionary, or a believing Jew. For within existentialism there are few resources to understand what happened at Treblinka, as witness Simone de Beauvoir's pallid observation that the book is justified, for it helps us to understand. Understand, yes; but what? Not that the humanity of man consists in his power to act even when all is futile. The freedom fighter declares. 'This revolt must show the world that at the very bottom of the abyss we have not despaired.'[38] Surely the story of Treblinka means that the power to act comes from the conviction that the historical future can be shaped by man, that things can be different and we can make them so. Hope is the soil of act. And it fulfils its own prophecies.

The Pattern of Modern Hoping

One of the striking things about the four examples we have reviewed is the emergence of a pattern of promise. Certain themes recur and, in fact, take on the semblance of a rhythmic movement. We shall attempt to trace out briefly the contours of this design and then use it as a framework for conversation with Christian hope.

1. Radical Evil

Modern hopers cannot be written off as utopians. They are not blind to the travail of the world and the portentous possibilities of future disaster. King knows the central fact of the black man's life of pain and the white man's hypocrisy, the futurist has his nightmares, the hobbit's pilgrimage is lived out in the shadow of doom, and no one has to tell the Treblinka revolutionary of what evil man is capable. Each has been to hell and back.

2. Future Focus

They know the horror of the times, but they are not mesmerized by it. Something wrenches their gaze away from the abyss and beyond it. They are not trapped in enervating fascination with the moment and its perils, they are free enough to look up and ahead. It is the future that breaks the grip of a demanding present.

3. Expectation

There is nothing in the nature of future-orientation that makes it hopeful. Some whose eyes are forward see a worse fate in store for our projects, historical cataclysm, heat death for the universe. But for the future-oriented with whom we are dealing, the end is not controlled by radical evil. While there is every possibility that the worst can happen, the future is an open one. Things can be different. Morning can come.

4. Evidence

Tillich observes, 'If a daydreamer expects to become something that has no relation to his present state . . . he is a fool . . . Where there is genuine hope, that for which we hope has already some presence.'[39] What rescues the modern hoper from daydreaming is the evidence he sees. Hope takes root in the soil of reality. There is just enough evidence of the 'not yet' in the 'already' to nourish expectation.

5. Change Agency

The kind of evidence which turns up the burners of hope is the power of men to mould events. Narrowed in range by the preconditioning past, crushed by the weight of radical evil, yet there is enough manoeuvring room in the 'now' to make a difference. Men are not pawns but men. And because they have been able to affect their present, they can seize their future as well.

6. Mandate

Where this rhythm of realism, promise and proof gains momentum, it presses towards a fulfilling deed. The prior ingredients form themselves into a mandate. Men who have tasted the possibility of a future which can be different are driven to work for it to be so. The surge ahead becomes 'hope in action'.

There is abroad in the land a new breed of hopers. They are men of sorrows acquainted with grief. Yet they know something more. They think in the idiom of a man whose politics and church building they might question, but whose 'rhythm' they would understand. His inscription, set over the doorway of the parish church of Staunton Harold in Leicestershire, England, reads:

In the yeare: 1653
when all thinges sacred were throughout the Nation
either demolisht or profaned,
Sir Robert Shirley Barronet
founded this Church;
whose singular praise it is
to have done the best things in the worst times
and
to have hoped them in the most calamitous

2. The Structure of Christian Hope

I

It is no accident that Christian hopers look with fraternal interest on the kind of modern hoper represented in our initial survey. This is true not only because there are obvious direct links, as in the case of Martin Luther King. The affinity lies in the structure that is shared by 'secular' and biblical perspectives. While contemporary hope and Christian hope cannot be translated into each other without residue, they do live in a common universe of discourse. It is important to discover that this is so. Not in order to claim that the best fruits of the modern spirit come from Christian seed—without the pastime of oneupmanship, there is a job for historical scholarship to explore the connexions, although that is not the task we have set for ourselves here. We want to see if there is a forum for conversation on the future between Christian and modern perspectives. Such a dialogue might open new vistas to each. And more, it might encourage a partnership among the future-oriented in building a habitable 'not yet'. To this end we examine the six components in the light of a Christian eschatology sensitive to that goal.

The Massive Fact of Evil

As in the contemporary eschatologies we have selected, so in Christian faith, there is no blinking the facts of man's plight. Christian eschatology is rooted in a sober appraisal of the desperation of the human condition. It is expressed in vivid imagery descriptive of the subversive work, in the world, of the powers of evil.

The *power of destruction* (damnation, sickness) is everywhere manifest in the sundered bonds between man and man, man and nature, man and himself, nature and itself. Neighbour lifts up the sword against neighbour, the child cannot put its hand over the asp's hole, man is torn in spirit and diseased in body, and the whole creation groans in travail.

At the centre of this universal rent is the final separation, death. Death at its deepest level is separation from God, the cutting off of man from life. The *power of death* threatens to deal the ultimate blow to the human pilgrimage.

The biblical eye that surveys this holocaust comes to rest on its source in man himself and the *power of sin*. It has no neat theory to explain the connexion between the disruptive self-will it sees in man and the turmoil to be found on the earth. But it stands convicted of its guilt and knows that its issue is destruction and death.

For the mystery that hangs hazelike over the battlefield of destruction, death and sin, the language of the demonic comes to hand. The strange elusive tempter, *provocateur* partner in crime is *the power of the devil*. The enigma has no final explanation, so the best that can be done is to point to its presence, name it, and even personify it, so that the personal struggle it evokes will be given its due.

This New Testament sight looks as deeply, if not more deeply, into the same abyss which grips the most sober of cynics and the most realistic of hopers.

'Straining Forward'

But it is not hypnotized by what it sees. Its eyes lift from the immediacies to the horizon ahead. Ernst Benz, commenting on the grip in which post-war philosophy and literature were held by the horrors experienced by an era of chaos, puts forcefully the freed range of the eyes of faith:

> The generation of thinkers who came to the fore after World War II suffered the fate of Lot's wife. She looked back upon burning Sodom and Gomorrah. She could not look away from the picture of decline and destruction. She became mesmerized by the abyss of human aberrations, . . . She got lost in the constricting numbness of fear and defeat and—she was converted into stone . . . it is time for us to look forward as Lot did.[1]

Christian vision, therefore, introduces a new ingredient into the sober review of the tragic givens. It sees them, but it is not in their grip. It can look honestly at what is, but is not captive to the *status quo*. It breaks up the neat calculus: The 'Now' is evil, the 'Now' is all, therefore all is evil; and declares: The 'Now' is not all there is; the new factor is the 'Not Yet'. The future shatters the spell of the 'Now'. The future is freedom. It breaks the chains of both the present and the past.

The pull exerted by the future on Christian seeing comes from the End of the Story, the Goal towards which the drama moves. Nourished in the tradition of Jewish messianism, the New Testament vision also views history as a tilt towards what will be. There is no other place to go, no

47

status quo ante or *status quo,* for nothing is so solidly rooted that it can resist the slide forward. While the *ultimate* future exercises the final pressure on the present, the *penultimate* 'not yet', the road that must be next traversed, is also part of the Christian future. In fact, as the next step, it looms as the most engrossing. In the moments of keenest anticipation of an immanent End, the New Testament writers are fixed on the importance of the historical tomorrow – they must get the word out, they must organize their community in the light of final glory, they must tell, celebrate and live their Story, in order to make the highway straight for the coming Lord. All of the penultimate strivings are gauged by the measuring rod of the finale and its urgency. But it is the day when the sun comes up for which they work.

Faith therefore races towards its destination, forgetting what lies behind . . . 'straining forward to what lies ahead' (Philippians 3 : 13)

Whetted Expectations

'Eat drink and be merry for tomorrow we die' – that is one way to view the future. The end is a threat, certain doom for all the bubbling life of the 'Now'. Therefore seize what you can before it's all over!

But there is another picture of tomorrow. Paul's letter continues, 'straining forward to what lies ahead, I press on towards the goal for the prize . . .' Faith's future-orientation is expectant about what lies up ahead. Faith shines with hope.

Actually, it is possible only for purposes of analysis to treat separately expectation and future-orientation. As in the case of the Philippian passage, so in all the other New Testament references to the 'Not Yet', there is no abstract interest in the future as such, with content afterward poured into it, as our catalogue of components might here suggest.

Rather, the future is the focus of faith precisely because of its hope. It is the joy of meeting Joy that turns the eye of the believer forward.

What is it that looms on the horizon? Here we must make some careful distinction. The first is, as earlier suggested, the difference between the ultimate and penultimate End, the 'eternal' Goal and temporal goals, the final Vision and its derivative visions.

The Final Vision

It is the 'One who comes' that climaxes the Christian story. At the centre of hope is the expectation of God's appearance. What has been hidden, ambiguous, tantalizingly unclear (and therefore evocative of the leap of faith) will be manifest. He who is Omega will take possession of what he is.

Christian talk about this disclosure races back and forth between its Christocentric commitments and the more universal language of 'God'. The One who comes is Christ. Yet it is also God. And why not both, who are in fact one and the same? The struggles over the Trinity are duplicated in eschatology. And the best we can say in the translucent language of the present, to describe a reality which is not now but will be, is to confess that the two will be one. What nonsense. But no more so than a futurist who tries to express what will be in the year 2000 in the categories of 1969. It can't be done. But those who believe in the future must try, and will try.

As secular men, we will stumble and struggle with the lush imagery in which the Storybook portrays the Disclosure. What is all this about coming on clouds, sitting on thrones, and the wounding of dragons – in one last desperate battle? Empirical men smile at the picture stories. But how else could eyes fixed on a futuristic vision tell about

49

what they see? They took the most vivid scenes of their present to portray the 'Not Yet'. They had to say it their way, as we must in ours. But let us honour the integrity of what they did, and learn what lies at its heart.

Viewed from the angle of *our* 'Now', what is luminous is the conviction that the One to whom both we and they share allegiance shall not be turned aside. The very worst that man can attempt against him will not succeed. He will be who he will be. He will come into his own. The End is the vindication of his promise, to dwell with his people, to know and be known.

In the Christian tale, the One who comes brings something with him. He is not alone. The King establishes his Kingdom.

The gifts of the King are a 'new heaven and a new earth', a city whose builder and maker is God. The streets are paved with gold and the walls are of jasper, the banquet table is spread, the halls resound with song, swords are beaten into ploughshares, wolf and lamb lie down together. This talk of the Kingdom is odder than the language about the King. What can it possibly mean for us?

At the heart of the rich symbolism of the End is the celebration of the promised unity of the world. Healing will happen! All the sundered relations within the cosmos shall be knit together. The powers of evil shall perish and *shalom* shall be.

This word is used to indicate all aspects of life in its full and God-given maturity; righteousness, truth, fellowship, peace, etc. This single word summarizes all the gifts of the messianic age; even the name of Messiah can simply be *shalom* (Micah 5: 5; Eph. 2: 14); the Gospel is a Gospel of *shalom* (Eph. 6: 15), and the God proclaimed in this Gospel can often be called the God of *shalom*. . . . The goal towards which God is working, i.e. the ultimate end of his mission, is the establishment of *shalom*, and this involves the realization of the full potentialities of all creation and its ultimate reconciliation and unity in Christ.[2]

How about the particulars of this vision? They too are telling a tale. The jewels are those they have seen on their kings, the laden tables those whose delights they have tasted or guessed, the swords destroyed are those from their armouries, the ploughs are from their fields, the lambs are from their folds, the wolves they have met in the woods. It is their world through and through. Heaven is furnished with the materials of earth as Feuerbach so rightly saw. But that is precisely the point. All the fragments of what is good and true and beautiful in their history are swept up by the divine hand and woven into the final tapestry. He brings it. But it is they who have made it. He does not import foreign stuff into the New Creation. It wears their label. The implications of this home-grown product for action in the 'Now' we shall presently explore. All we are after at the moment is to see the meaning of the vision's furnishings in eschatological perspective. It is that the tiniest token of personal, historical, cosmic value will not fade from view. The Preserver and Restorer builds a Kingdom out of the treasures of the earth. He makes all things new, but what he makes new is our home.

The Penultimate Vision

What will be in the End leaves its footprints in the soil of our historical tomorrows. Not with the same finality and clarity, but there nevertheless.

The God who is in Christ waits for us at a rendezvous point out ahead. As he is with us today, so he will be tomorrow. Of course, we shall not meet him 'face to face' around the corner of a 1970. But he will be there, seen 'through a glass darkly'. That is why we look forward to even the most dismal of historical futures. We may die, but he shall not. We are not driven to despair and flight at the prospect of defeat for our plans and dreams. The one future that matters – his – is secure.

Where he is, there his glory will be as well. And he has promised to be with us 'even unto the End'. The 'glory of the Lord' that visionaries have seen coming into history is the breakthrough of *shalom*. Yes, still harassed by powers that do not know that the game is up; but, for all that, genuine signs, portents, firstfruits. Christians discern, celebrate and participate in the earnests of *shalom* wherever swords are beaten into ploughshares, wherever the oppressed receive justice, the hungry are fed, wounds are bound up, pain and death are contested, the prisoner is released and creation's travail is eased. Because he will be there in the historical future, his rainbow stretches over that horizon too. Men have a right to dream and to pray, 'Your Kingdom come on earth', because where his presence is, there will his power be.

How easily his promise to be and to do is transformed into something else by men too ready to bend Christian hope to fit their own longings. Thus hope is turned into an escalator theory of progress by which mankind is transported into an untrammelled future. But Christian dreaming is done with its eyes open. Its hope is sobered by what it sees of the continued work of the powers of evil, and what it knows of immodest claims for the Kingdom that end in idolatry or despair. Hope soars, but with its ballast of realism. Its appetite is whetted for new levels of historical possibility that could be signs of *shalom*. But precisely because they represent an advance, they are that much more vulnerable to the blandishments of 'the devil', who does his most effective work among the righteous, who is capable of subtler forms of sin and of a destruction and death more disastrous where achievements are greater ('the bigger they are, the harder they fall').

The Evidence of Things not Seen

Oscar Cullmann traces the eschatological fervour of the early Church to events that have already happened, a point of view that distinguishes Christian expectation from that of other religions:

> 'the hope of final victory is so much the more vivid because of the unshakably firm conviction that the battle that decides the victory has already taken place'.[3]

If Cullmann is right, Christian hope may be nearer in spirit to the secular hopes we have examined than to the eschatologies of other religious communities. Like the former, hope is secured against fantasy and wishful thinking by its anchor in the 'already'. It is based on evidence. the End has already come – in Jesus Christ.

In this one man, healing has happened. The vision of a world at one with itself is earthed. Where he goes, torn bodies, minds and spirits are knit together. The broken bonds between men are mended, the seas are stilled and peace is made with God. The waves of the absolute Future have rolled up on our own shores here and now. He is our *Shalom*.

To grasp the significance of these awesome events we must look more closely at the career of the man from Nazareth.

Done by a Man

We saw how secular hopes are tied to the conviction that the future can be affected by human action. When men see they can make a difference to what will be, they look up and ahead. Christian hope has the same roots. The evidence that emboldens is the work of Christ, what this man did to change the future.

The Story does not mute the horror that everywhere is

to be found in the world. In fact, as we have tried to show, it gives a more honest and profound report of the powers of evil than alternative assessments of the wretchedness of the earth. But the central conviction of the Christian faith is that these enemies have met their match. Up until the Happening, the powers ruled unchallenged. They were masters of human destiny. The future belonged to them and over its door they nailed up a 'No exit' sign. But this man tore it down.

At each step along his pilgrimage towards the future, he confronted the powers and vanquished them. At the outset of his ministry he faced down his Adversary and at its close he repelled again his last ditch assaults. He routed the powers that disrupt the bodies and minds of men. He confronted and overruled the powers that cause men to cower before the sound and fury of nature. He lived for God and neighbour, defeating in the depths of his own self the sin that infects the human will and act.

He died the same way, bearing the burden of guilt that had thrust the race to the ground. And on Easter morning he overcame the last enemy, death.

What mankind could not do, this man did. In Adam all died, but in this second Adam is new life to be found. Here is the first of a new race. He loosened the grip of the powers on the future. He pushed open its door. Now we can go through!

Faith sees, by way of the New Testament pictures of this man's career, what the Story is all about. It is a tale of an open future. In its ultimate dimension, it is the assurance of things hoped for. The mission of God cannot be turned aside; the powers of evil go down for the count; *Shalom* will be. In its penultimate dimension, it is whetted expectations for what can be in our time and our history. Because he pioneered, we can follow. Because he overcame the worst mauling the world could manage, he makes it possible for us to dare trace his steps over the same terrain. Yes, the lions still roar and reptiles still crawl along that trail, but the wild animals have been caged and the poison has been drawn from the fangs. The eerie powers no longer control the road up ahead.

There are radical implications to be drawn from this open future. It means that our straining forward is no exercise in futility. The future has been won by a man. And we too are men. Because of what he did, we can act towards the future and shape it. Men can make a difference, in time; yes, and in eternity as well. An open future means that what will be depends on what we will make it to be.

What Promethean arrogance! Or at the very least Pelagian! What is the difference between such bold talk and a pretentious humanism that asserts that:

> I am the master of my fate:
> I am the captain of my soul.

The difference lies in the grounding of Christian expectation. 'Faith is the assurance of things hoped for.' Faithful hope finds its evidence at a key point in the cosmic story, in this man, Jesus. Here is where the powers met their match. Here it happened once and for all. Without this angle of vision on the conquered and the conquerer, we wander aimlessly along the trail, frightened by the noises we hear and the sights we see. But faith perceives in the *shalom* event the clearing of the way. It is our window into the future.

Again, because faithful hope takes up a viewing position of history from its centrepoint, it sees another dimension of the action that goes on there and beyond. In and through this very human struggle with the powers of evil, it perceives the work of Another. How to report this co-presence to others who take up different stations has always been an enigma. It has been pretty clear, however, what it does not want to say it sees. It does not give out tales of a god walking around on earth in human disguise. Very early in its life the Church concluded that Jesus was no heavenly apparition devoid of full-blooded humanity. It rejected Docetism.

But equally unsatisfying it found Ebionism in all its forms – the idea that in Jesus we have to do with the most hard-working, wise and loving of all men – period! How does this reductionism square with the conviction that 'God was in Christ reconciling . . .'?

After centuries of puzzlement, experimentation and controversy, the Christian community hammered out at Nicaea and Chalcedon what was to become one of its central theses. The way through to the End was pioneered by the Christ who was truly man, truly God, truly one. With all its ambiguity and restlessness, this strange duality made more sense than the neat and packaged alternatives of over-deifying and over-humanizing. The future has been opened for us through a man's labour's of love by the grace of God.

The gracious underside of human effort is no static reality. The divine action is not limited to its entry point in history. It is a genuine breakthrough which transforms the whole character of time. In a Christic world, all human labour directed towards the building of *shalom* is seen by Christian eyes as the work of man done by God's grace. He lives in our action. We must return in the succeeding section to this point so crucial in both of its implications – the celebration of human creativity and its grounding in the divine life – for the orientation of Christian faith in an era of rapid secularization. For the time being, we simply affirm the Christian commitment to man's power to shape his own future by the presence of One who makes it possible.

Action towards the Future

The preceding ingredients brewed by Christian hope are an explosive mix. They are the stuff of which 'eschatological revolutionaries' are made, as Bloch, George Williams, Benz, and others have shown.[4] Aware of radical evil embodied in the ecclesiastical and social Establishment set against them, yet drawn by a future which stood in judgement on the givens, one that could be hastened by their own effort to close the gap, left-wing elements of the Reformation and splinter movements in Christianity sought to wrench the structures of society into conformity with their vision.

Action towards the future may also take intra-mural form. Instead of striking out at oppressive social, political and economic conditions, the internal life of the Church is made to mirror the End. Thus the New Testament communities sought to create a fabric of mutuality in which the outcast, the orphan, the widow, the poor, the hungry, the stranger, the prisoner, the slave found a care and dignity within the household of faith that reflected the final divine design. Here in the Church would be a foretaste of the time to come in which the meek would inherit the earth. When the Church began to settle down in later decades of waning apocalyptic, the Montanists recalled the Church to its first vision, putting it, however, through the filter of gnostic emphasis on the second-class character of the world of time and space.

An intense eschatology may also produce a fervant evangelism, as Hans Margull has demonstrated.[5] Early Christians saw their missionary task intimately related to the climax of history. Their call was to preach to the nations, not only before the End would come, but in order that it might. The Word had to be spread to the ends of the earth to prepare the way for the coming of the King.

57

Our task here is not to trace the effects that a full-blooded eschatology has had in history, but to note its power to evoke action and to ask what kind of action it might mean for us. In each era in which it has been given its course, its interpretation has been influenced by factors characteristic of that time. Thus the form that eschatological productivity took in New Testament times – missionary preaching and embodiments of intra-Church *shalom* – is directly related to the expectations of an imminent End which allowed little time for anything but preparing the beach-head among the faithful, and 'sounding the alarm' to those outside. In our own setting in which the time-table of the End has under-gone revision, the character of the action must also be broadened. The whole range of human and natural life, not only life within the walls of the Christian community, is brought under the eschatological mandate. The highway that must be straightened for the Lord's coming runs out beyond the Church into the world. His beach-head is everywhere. Faithful eschatological action calls into ques-tion every social structure that militates against the final Design, and struggles to mould all relations between man and man, man and nature, nature within nature, and be-tween man-nature and God, in conformity with its vision.

The outcome of authentic eschatology is action. Weighted by the agonies of the world and a penitence that knows its own involvement in them, hope struggles to its feet and gets them on the road ahead. It knows about a man who has gone this way before, who marched off the map making the forbidding unknown a trail of promise. To hope is to be a follower of Jesus.

II

Secularization and Hope

We have examined Christian eschatology by way of elements that link it with modern hopers. We want now to bring together the components of Christian hope around the focus of a contemporary issue with which the Church must come to terms in all sectors of its life and thought – God or man? The process of secularization has catapulted this alternative to the foreground of church reflection. How do we speak about God in the setting of this-worldliness, and in a time when man is increasingly able to do by himself the tasks he has assigned to Deity or sought through the agency of religion? How do we relate to modern hopers whose expectations are solely intra-historical, who wait for and work for, and sometimes claim, the realization of their Kingdom on earth?

Implicit in the design sketched so far are two premises that relate to these questions. 1. Secularization is to be celebrated. Men should turn their eyes to this world in this time when its anguishes cry out for ministration, its exhilarations invite joyful participation. Men should come of age, finding solutions to their problems without the club or crutch of religious idea, rituals, institutions. 2. Secularization is the work of God himself. He wants men to attend to the awesome responsibilities of this world and not run for cover. On Jericho roads, the faithful do not hand out tracts, they bind up wounds. It is God who presses man from the nest so that he may take his future into his own hands. To affirm the process of secularization is not the same thing as wedding oneself to the product, secularism. Christians have a story to tell about the One who calls man to servanthood, joy and hope in his world.

The problem we face in modern eschatology is to state

this dual commitment in such a way that both human venture and its divine grounding and goal are given their full freedom.

This is not the first time in Christian history that the question, 'God or man?' has been faced. It has kept awake at night some of the best minds of the Church as they puzzled over the meaning of Christ, the Church, the sacraments, the Bible and the Christian life. We shall draw on the insights that emerged in these struggles, and one in particular, variously identified as the principle of complementarity, hypostasis, paradox, mystical union, double agency, etc.

We have already noted that early in its life the Christian community wrestled with its fundamental identity in the debates on the person of Christ. Rejecting reductionism, it has since sought to do its Christological work within the framework of a commitment to full deity, full humanity and unity.

While there is no simple continuity between Christ and the continuing vehicles of his life, the same problem did recur in the struggle to understand them. Thus, partisans, ancient and modern, have insisted that the Church is essentially a human group organized for pious purposes and comprehensible in sociological categories alone. Others have whisked her off the earth with pretensions to supernatural status. Against these contentions is set the conviction that the Church is not a one-dimensional reality, but a body of people with all its frailties that lives by the 'laws' of sociological understanding, but at one and the same time the Body of Christ. Again, a sacramental controversy that has raged between 'low church' opinions, that view the transactions as aids to conviction or fellowship, and 'high church' positions, that transform them into supernatural entities, is increasingly challenged by an understanding which affirms the earthiness of the action and elements, yet sees them as genuine vehicles of a loving Presence. In the effort to grasp the significance of the Bible, the polarization between those who have collapsed it into the category of great literature and those who have turned it into a lump of divinity that ought not to be touched by human hand or tool is left behind by a perspective ready and willing to acknowledge its human agency and to open it to the most vigorous of literary scrutiny, but committed to listening for the Word that comes through the words. And in the continuing contest between Pelagians and predestinarians, another option seeks to acknowledge the paradox of divine initiative and responsibility in the Christian life in the Pauline categories of 'It is I, yet not I, but Christ . . .'. Jonathan Edwards's attempt to express this inexpressible duality of grace and freedom by the 'principle of complementarity' points to the direction in which the historical struggles move, and sets the scene for our own attempt to work at the question in eschatology:

> In efficacious grace we are not merely passive, nor yet does God do *some*, and we do the *rest*. But God does all, and we do all. God produces all, and we act all. For that is what he produces, viz. our own acts. God is the only proper author and fountain; we only are the proper actors.[6]

Four Points of Intersection

1. Shalom

We have described the goal of history in terms of *shalom*, employing an image of which the World Council of Churches' inquiry on the Missionary Structure of the Congregation has made creative use.[7] Underscoring the healing of every fracture in creation, as this is anticipated in Old Testament prophecy and apocalyptic as well as in New

61

Testament expectations, *shalom* rescues eschatology from abortive conceptions of Christian hope which narrow salvation to the soul and/or propose its vertical flight to another world. This false counsel ignores God's intent to mend *all* torn relationships, including those between man and man, wolf and lamb. Christian participation in, and testimony to, the movement towards the divine goal presses the believer into work for those structures in nature and history which reflect that wholeness. The prayer, 'Thy Kingdom come on earth' means what it says. King's struggle for black justice, the futurologists' concern over thermonuclear and genetic developments, and revolutions for freedom in concentration camps and classrooms cannot be declared off-limits to Christian eschatology. Hope is earthed.

But then, is there another 'No trespassing' sign? Is God's design restricted to this world? Is hope only intra-historical? The richness and freedom of Christian eschatology cannot be so impoverished. No more than Ebionism can do justice to the stature of Christ, nor Pelagianism to the Christian life, nor sociological analysis alone define the nature of the Church, nor literary instruments measure the full meaning of the Bible, can a terrestrial horizon limit the range of Christian expectation. There is a plus factor to be dealt with in eschatology, as in Christology, ecclesiology and soteriology. We grope for it when we describe the Christian vision of fulfilment as a 'new creation' and a 'new heaven and earth' rather than as perfection within the limits of the given creation, heaven and earth. We wrestle with ways of describing it, finding the 'end of history' more meaningful than 'above history' or 'in history', thus relating the vision to the historical process, yet making no final claims for, or putting no ultimate confidence in, historical realizations.

We get a clue to it in its New Testament firstfruits, the

resurrection of Jesus, characterized by continuity with the life of men, yet in a different key. And further, there is one fundamental factor about history that drives the Christian eye over the horizon: the powers of evil. As long as history remains history, and free men are called to decisions, human incurvature will do its work, rendering ambiguous the most laudatory achievements. If there is to be any final conquest, history itself will have to be transformed. And this is the scenario which hope finds in biblical faith, a transhistorical goal in which sin, fissure, demon and death receive their due.

As Reinhold Niebuhr has sought to teach us (how quickly we forget, in our current upsurge of hope!), the biblical refusal to identify the Kingdom with any phenomenon preserves the hoper from the self-righteous fury and fanaticism of the 'true believer' who knows that the Kingdom has arrived in his formulations, feelings or social constructs – and from the despair and flight that results when utopian commitments are frustrated by the stubborn facts of life.

While a *shalom* that evokes historical action and is embodied in it, yet not exhausted by it, does open the future more faithfully than simple this-worldly versions of eschatology, it is not this pragmatic criterion alone that establishes its validity. In the final analysis, anything less than a dialectical view of the End is less than a full reading of the Christian Story. In its complete orb, especially as New Testament accents are heard against the background of the Old Testament arena of historical and cosmic promise, the Christian vision lives within the arcs of both penultimate and ultimate.

There will be great pressure in a secular age to cut future-talk back to the empirical language in which it comfortably nests. And there will be noises made on the right by other-worldly types frightened by the times into flight to the transcendent. But a determined eschatology responsible to its roots in the Christian Story must fight its way by these detours to an affirmation of the full range of the future reducible neither to its tomorrows nor to Tomorrow.

2. *The Person and Work of Christ*

We have sought to interpret in Section 1 the central event in the Christian drama with full freedom for human and divine action. At the risk of some repetition, but in the interests of seeing all the intersecting points, we look again at the duality in the career of Jesus.

Through the lens of a recapitulation view of the Atonement that traces its lineage to Irenaeus, Christ is seen in active struggle with the powers that control man's future. At each turn, the contest lost by men is won by Christ. While the timid will draw back from the vivid pictorial in which this claim is set forth, there is such good news being shouted here that all the quibbles as to how it may be expressed pale into insignificance. The door of the future has been thrust open. The man Jesus was the first to break the spell of forlornness. An Adam like us, by his victory, a second Adam, here is the first of a new race. Because he pioneered, we can find the way. Discipleship is following him towards the future no longer closed, but bursting with the promise of at-one-ment with its love.

As with Irenaeus, so with any modern version of a pioneering Jesus, Atonement is interlaced with Incarnation. It is true man that does the work.

If God appeared like a bolt from the blue to whelm his enemies, there is no hope for humanity. Man remains the infant who is provided for by a benevolent paternalism, a 'big Daddy' who bails him out of his troubles. A divine triumphalism is not a word to a generation coming of age. And, more important, it is a false report of the life of a man who was tempted, bled and died as we do, and of the Father who loved the prodigal enough to allow him to come to himself, and loved a son enough to absent himself in the time of final maturation. Incarnation means that we have to do with a real human being who went the route for us.

But it is Incarnation of Another. Here again is this gnawing, racking mystery. Full man, yes; living out a fully human life – no superman that glided benignly through his contests, with otherworldly wands to wave – sweating, crying, doubting, bleeding, dying. But in his suffering we see a Sufferer. What more can we say? This is the God-Man.

3. Christ at Work in the World

The divine – human polarity is met in the present life of Christ as well as the New Testament events. Here come too the tempting alternatives. One lively notion put forward by Thomas Altizer declares for a metamorphosis in which the sacred becomes the profane, the divine disappearing into history at the death of Jesus, becoming an 'Incarnate Word' honoured when God's death is trumpeted and the man of faith immerses himself in the secular. Another option is the familiar invitation to fly into the arms of a Christ who dwells above. And there is the point of view which does indeed insist that history is the theatre of divine action, but views it as a chessboard on which God's grace manipulates events and men are pawns in a grand design.

As in other points in the eschatological pilgrimage, so too here in our 'Now' the dialectic cannot be smoothed out to accommodate either secular sensitivities or steamroller versions of God's action. We have spoken of a divine–human co-determination, in which the integrity of each partner, and the unity of both, are affirmed. Thus whether we look at present events or future historical and natural possibilities, we are talking about processes for which man is responsible, and without human efforts they are not, or will not be realized. The present fragments of *shalom* are man's work and tomorrow's possibilities which can only come when man seizes them. But forward venture towards *shalom* is surely by God's grace. The Christian life testifies to the mystery of the divine tide which, though we must take it at the flood, is of God's ordering. To try to ferret out the mechanism of this unity in duality is to stumble into various synergisms which parcel out responsibilities to each, sometimes with a special nod towards God – he is senior partner and we are junior – which only serves to cast suspicion on the full participation of both divine and human agencies. The best we can do is to acknowledge that once again we have run up into a reality that cannot be pressed into the narrow canons of formal logic. It needs something that shatters our conventional wisdom. But in doing so, it puts feet on the path towards the future in a way the neatly devised alternatives cannot do, and thus proves wiser in its foolishness than the wisdom of men.

4. The Finale

As we dealt in the first section with the historical trans-historical aspect of the End, we focus here on the interlaced question of divine and human initiative. Can man build it or does God bring it? To say than man can bring it either in time or eternity (usually argued in our era in the former idiom, although there are examples in Christian history of the latter in the so-called sect movements) is to put God at the beck and call of man, thus violating the divine integrity, or dismissing him as a serious factor in the Kingdom's coming. To say that God brings it without the involvement of man is to persist in the imperialist categories which controlled social and religious concepts and structures for too long. In order to break out of this trap, and to see fresh dimensions of the Christian story as well, we have worked at an understanding of the end of the End in the categories of divine–human complementarity.

The Kingdom is, in a crucial sense, man-made. The rhetoric of the social Gospel pointed to this, but did it undialectically. The city abuilding – penultimate and ultimate – is composed of human material. The foretastes in time of a healed creation are the work of man. But the same is true of the Kingdom in its fulness. We have interpreted the role of man's work in the goal of creation as providing the building blocks for the new heaven and new earth. What shape it takes is determined by God, but without the building blocks of man there is no structure. Human effort, therefore, is the offering to God of the fruit of its labour for the design he brings to birth. Each act of man that is fit material has eternal significance, for it will take its place in the divine configuration. 'Do not lay up for yourselves treasures on earth, where moth and rust consume and where thieves break in and steal, but lay up for yourselves treasures in heaven, where neither moth nor rust consumes and where thieves do not break in and steal' (Matthew 6 : 19–20).

We and our products are the stones, but he is the Master-builder. To honour the integrity of the divine in the consummation of creation is to accord him the right, in our frail formulations, to be God. To be God in the culminating transaction is to have the power of self-determination, to come not at man's initiative (hence the weakness of notions of the End that allow man to determine his coming, in fact, even midwife its birth), but at God's, to seal as well the final fate of the expiring powers and to transmute the gifts of men into the radical new idiom of a resurrected world.

Of course, when we talk about grand finales on the outermost rim of the future we must be ready to smile at our fancies, for that is what our groping, embarrassed awkward formulations are. But the myths of apocalypse have stirred our imaginations, stretched perspectives and fired more than a few eschatological revolutionaries. We do not apologize for the extravagant language of the New Testament or for our own feeble speculations, for they can open up 'alternative futures' which mobilize for action. Thus, to believe that the Absolute Future includes a component of man's making stamps human effort with an ultimate concern of utter clarity. And to the question of 'the future of the dead', answer is made that no granule of the good, the true or the beautiful is lost to God or remains unfulfilled.

It is not only we, of course, who will smile at our constructs and speculations. Secular men have little time for talk of divine crafting, and less for grand finales. That is why the tip-point of our mission will be the words and deeds that build our common historical future. But while living in the times, faith is not beholden to them. The Christian is a free man. He is free enough to tell his tale even when the world has tuned him out. It would not be the first time that such news was considered foolishness. And when it is, faith-talk – and in this case, hope-talk – may increasingly take on the character of the *disciplina arcani* (secret devotion), a hidden jewel that shines best in the catacombs of the Christian community. Christians share with enthusiasm in building the future with their fellowmen. But the secret seeds of that impulse are not lightly scattered on inhospitable terrain. They are celebrated in its underground life in the code language of a City of Hope and its Builder.

In the next chapter we carry on a conversation within the

68

code community. As the Church gets re-acquainted with its almost lost language of hope, an array of new eschatological theologies are making their appearance. Their influence is already apparent in some of the themes developed in this chapter. We select three pacesetters, listen to their main accents, probe them, and enlarge upon some of the themes here developed.

3. Contemporary Conversation in Hope

The 1967 forecast of a religious periodical that the new eschatological accents bid fair soon to occupy the centre of theological discussion seems well on the way to fulfilment. Some will, of course, dismiss it as the latest fad, in a pop-oriented forum too captive to journalist manipulation. There is certainly some truth in that. However, the new eschatological theologies have a much deeper rootage in responsible Christian thought than other sensationalist flurries. Also the linkage with an array of secular hopers and with the background of a future-oriented time suggests that is is a serious and lasting development.

We select three of the most articulate and influential voices in the current eschatological chorus.[1] They have had their effect on the position outlined in the previous chapter. But there are significant differences as well. We shall examine the points of view of Jürgen Moltmann, Teilhard de Chardin and Harvey Cox appreciatively and critically, in the hope of moving forward the dialogue on the future.

(i) Jürgen Moltmann

> The eschatological is not one element *of* Christianity, but it is the medium of Christian faith as such, the key in which everything in it is set, the glow that suffuses everything here in the dawn of an expected new day.[2]

The impact of Moltmann's own work, *Theology of Hope*, has added force to his assertion of eschatology's central place. The Christian community can be grateful to him for bringing to the foreground a theme which addresses itself directly to a future-oriented time.

While Christocentric through and through, Moltmann's perspective has taken form in running dialogue with modern hopers, and especially with the 'esoteric Marxism' of Ernst Bloch.[3] The revolutionary impulse in Christian eschatology is tracked to its source, and an effort is made to recover it without the distortions introduced by millenarian movements, and free of the illusions of Marxist and other 'secularized' apocalypse. Moltmann also hones the critical edge of eschatology in debate with existential theologies, notably Bultmann's, which he believes have so interiorized, individualized and 'presentized' the Gospel that its revolutionary teeth have been pulled. And it has been further tamed by vaporizing the historical and cosmic terrain in which the biblical story is enacted. He takes issue as well with various forms of 'transcendental eschatology' (including Barth's) which, he feels, fail to take the future seriously.

Major Accents in a Theology of Promise

The Old Testament rhythm of promise and fulfilment, shaped by Abraham and Mosaic expectation, by the Exodus and prophetic testimony, lays down the lines of a biblical eschatology. The Covenant community looked forward to a future in company with the Yahweh who would shatter swords, bring justice to the oppressed and vindicate his chosen. Expectations of things to come were related to past events of either fulfilment or frustration, although always analogically only, since the God who is full of surprises and free enough to 'repent' and change his mind can bring fresh dimensions of *shalom* into his people's midst. What is a complex of 'Israel-centred' historical hopes becomes stretched towards a universal blessing and cosmic healing in later prophetic and apocalyptic forecasts.. These Old Testament motifs become the material for the formation of a New Testament eschatology.

The promises discerned by Israel are confirmed and transfigured in the coming of Jesus. Their fulfilment is secured in the cross and resurrection. The cross discloses the full horror of the world's captivity to the powers of evil, and the divine solidarity with it. But life triumphs over death on Easter morning. What is yearned for in the Old Covenant is granted in the New in the promissory act of Christ's resurrection:

> . . . because God has the power to quicken the dead and call into being things that are not, therefore the fulfilment of his promise is possible, and because he has raised Jesus from the dead, therefore the fulfilment of his promise is certain.[4]

By the resurrection the future belongs to Christ and is, therefore, the 'future of Christ'. He is the one who comes towards us. With him he brings righteousness, life and a Kingdom in which the shattered creation will be made new and whole, the dead will be raised, and God will be all in all.

In the rays of this light shining from the End, history is exposed for what it is, corrupt and in travail. The vision contradicts and calls into radical question all that is. The effect of this juxtaposition of fulfilment with the frustration of immediacy makes the Christian hoper restless with the *status quo*.[5] Rather than leading to passivity, the gap be-

72

tween what is and what will be drives towards action. Hope mobilizes for mission.

Mission is a service of the *eschaton* which strives to bend reality towards the new horizon, to prepare the way for its coming, to 'make straight the highway' for the approaching Lord. Herein lies its revolutionary character, for hope is never satisfied with what is. It presses beyond even the resting-places in history to which secular eschatologies are tempted to retreat because its gaze is fixed upon an ever-receding 'yonder'. Moreover, to be assured that man's last enemy, death, cannot, in a post-Easter world, destroy the grounds of hope, as it must do in secularized eschatologies, is to be given further impetus to act towards the future. The reason is that the Christian hoper has been freed of both despair and the temptation to look for 'extraterritorial' areas of human existence immune to death.[6]

What of the impingement of the future on the present? The End is known in the here-and-now as the breakthrough of promise. Thus in the Church the Spirit works in baptism to graft men into a community of promise where they are nourished in hope by the Supper, and hear the coming future proclaimed in the Word. The Kingdom works proleptically also in possibilities that are opened up in history for freedom, justice, peace and righteousness, and the aspirations and struggles of men towards this renewal. But these trailmarkers towards the future of Christ in both Church and world must be understood to be, in the strictest sense, promissory. Cultic Christianity has beguiled men from history and the future by collapsing the presence of Christ into sacramental immediacies. And the little hopes for historical renewal of men have been confused by utopianism, messianism, and legalism with the fulfilment which God only can bring at the End.

An eschatology which stirs men to revolutionary im-

73

patience with what is, in the light of an End begun in the resurrection of Jesus is a perspective on the future. In addition to being a faithful reading of the biblical hope, it keeps history moving towards the fresh realization of ever new possibilities. Its attempt to be faithful to the Christian Story and its efforts to relate to the living issues of our time make the 'theology of hope' a force to be reckoned with in the years ahead.

Some Critical Questions

The debt that many current re-formulations of eschatology owe to Jürgen Moltmann is great indeed. His theology of promise has had a strong influence in the perspective taking shape in these pages. But questions tax, and uncertainties there are as well. Some come from unclarity of formulation, and others from the developing nature of Moltmann's position, both of which sometimes result in diametrically opposed interpretations and criticisms.[7] Still others have to do with disagreements of greater or lesser consequences. We explore four of the latter that rise out of the conception of Christian futurity set forth in Chapter 2.

1. The 'Already – Not Yet' Rhythm of Christian Eschatology

Is Moltmann's characterization of the 'already' that streams towards the 'not yet' a full report of New Testament commitments? He points unmistakably to the fountainhead in Jesus Christ. What about its flow? Do we hear of the work of Christ and the Kingdom in the time before the End?

Moltmann speaks of the earnests of the *eschaton* splayed by the Spirit through the preaching of the Word and the sacramental life. He also alludes to the genuine 'possibilities' in history for greater humanizing. And, of course, he seeks to impel the hoper towards revolutionary historical action.

However, the earnests of the Kingdom are inroads of promise which adumbrate, but are not in the full sense of the word *firstfruits* of, what is to come. the Kingdom appears as an arc that reaches from the resurrection of Christ over history and cosmos to its touchdown point at the resurrection of the dead. A world so bereft of the 'thermal current' of eschatological grace at work in the present is difficult to square with the Christian drama. It is not only the *promise* of Christ that breaks in proleptically but his real *presence* and power; not just the 'whiff' of what is to come but an authentic foretaste.

Surely one reason for Moltmann's reluctance to speak in more forcefully biblical terms about the present work of Christ by the Spirit is related to his suspicion of current presentative eschatologies. He sees both cultic and existential varieties calling the believer out of the theatre of his historical responsibility and away from the future to private and churchly engagements of immediacy. But the problem lies not in the concern for the 'Now', but in the reduction of the Story to the 'Now'. It is further distorted in present-oriented eschatologies by individualizing and ecclesiasticizing. Parochialism is corrected by stretching the horizon of faith to its future, corporate, and worldly perimeters, not by replacing one reductionism with another.

There seems to be another factor at work in Moltmann's eschatology which contributes to its timidity about the present work of Christ, and also to the problem that we shall next explore, the role of the human act in the eschatological drama: the apparent transposition of a forensic understanding of justification by faith into a futurist context. The vertical relationship has been tilted horizontally, with the characteristics of the former re-appearing in the new setting. God's gracious love bending in forgiveness towards the sinner becomes God's healing mercy coming towards his sin-sick creation out of the future. As the former evokes a faith that is busy in love, so the latter elicits from the believer a hope which expresses itself in revolutionary response. Saving grace, however, interpreted essentially as 'pardon' in the vertical encounter, appears in parallel fashion as 'promise' in the horizontal one. What is missing in the reading of the personal transaction of justification, as other traditions in both the Reformation and Catholic Christianity have sought to show, is grace, understood as *power in*, as well as *pardon of*, the sinner. There are processes of holiness and maturation that are real possibilities in the Christian life. The same corrective must be applied to an eschatology which stresses so radically the assurance of the Kingdom which shines on us from afar, but does not see the grace which leaves its trail in history towards the promise, a Kingdom which in foretaste is powerfully at work now, albeit in a fragment form that yearns for completion. The conquest of the powers of evil by Jesus means that his resurrecting grace has been turned loose in a Christic world. Hope ranges over that world with eager longing to discern the traces of that renewing power, to company with a lively Presence and to celebrate it. No matter how tenuous and ambiguous such realizations are, how laced with the possibilities of regress by dint of the powers of evil that still prowl, such firstfruits should be welcomed for what they are. Particularly is this true when we consider the further dimension of their activity. On pragmatic grounds, as we have seen from our review of modern hopers, men need to believe that tomorrow can be better than today, if they are to be moved to action towards it. And in the eschatological perspective we have been sketching, such a need has its foundations in reality. History is not 'godforsaken', illumined only by light from its End. It is also the theatre of God's present glory. Because this is so, men have a right to hope for real signs of *shalom* in time and space. The muting of this kind of historical expectation raises questions about the hopefulness of a 'theology of hope'.[8]

2. *Human Agency in Eschatology*

The divine prevenience is given full accent in Moltmann's eschatology. Hope is rooted in the raising of Jesus from the dead and the establishment of the glory of the Lord in the *eschaton*. Note is taken of eschatologies that stress the role of man in the redemption of the world, and their 'activistic messianism' and 'legalism' are rejected. In fact, Moltmann suggests that Paul's controversy with the Judaism of the Torah may, at bottom, involve the eschatological issue. 'Promise in the form of gospel, or promise in the form of law – that is the question.'[9]

There is no room in the New Testament promise for an eschatological Pelagianism. God will be God, and the divine initiative must be honoured. But there is a difference between the freedom of God to be God and the assertion of a divine triumphalism. Traditional formulations of God's action developed in a patriarchal era tend to succumb to the ascendancy-submission patterns of such a culture. The Lord of creation and redemption, like the lord of the manor and the household, was viewed with de Gaulle-like grandeur. But 'Big Daddy is dead', as the revolutions of the black, the poor, the young, the woman, the aged, the new nation, are increasingly making clear. The coming of age of legions of VLPs (very little persons) means throwing off the yoke of the VIPs who for so long have perpetuated autocracy. Movement is from monologue to dialogue, from paternalism to co-determination.

Theological formulations captive to old cultural categories must come in for serious re-examination. Does the ascendancy-submission framework, in which traditional conception of God's action were often cast, do justice to the Christian Story? The influence of this framework is apparent in some Reformation interpretations of justification by faith in which divine and human are polarized. In these eschatologies human agency is suspect. Moltmann's reluctance to speak of the present ferment of the Kingdom is one expression of this. The other is his inability to integrate into his eschatology the human factor. The 'big Daddy' posture is still a controlling theme.

The reaction against an old imperialism may lead to a new one. The intransigency of a monolith breeds a despair that insists on the death of all opposition and the establishment of a new autocracy in which the 'outs' becomes the 'ins'. Student revolt is met by police truncheons, and the rallying cry ceases to be co-determination and becomes instead student hegemony. The legitimate aspirations of black power and participation are met with white hatred and guns, and the result is a desperate black messianism. In theology the same processes are currently at work. When a rigid traditionalism turns a deaf ear to the new humanism that lifts up the dignity and role of man in the design of redemption, despair with the Establishment takes the form of 'death of God' theologies, 'death of Church' ecclesiologies and 'death of norm' moralities. If we do not take serious steps in both culture and faith to re-assess the role of human agency we have only ourselves to blame for the rise of new autocracies.

A regnant eschatology that makes no place for the partnership of man can expect to hear louder and louder noises being made about man as the controller of his own future. Already there are signs of it. But this alternative is as futile as the divine triumphalism against which it protests. An old modernism that sought to 'build the Kingdom on earth' makes little sense to men today who live close to radical evil, and to a Christian tale that knows as well the limits of history. What eschatology desperately needs is a re-formulation that honours fully the action of man in his pilgrimage towards the 'Not Yet', while preserving the evidence and initiative of God and the paradoxical working of his grace in, with and under human action.

This exceedingly difficult task must be close to the top of the agenda of modern eschatology. Christian thought must give it the same attention that is commanded in former struggles with the divine-human paradox in Christology, ecclesiology, soteriology, etc. That is why the summary of the general theology of hope here developing was keyed to this question in the second section of the last chapter. We offer that as a groping effort to speak to the issue and as an alternative to Moltmann's theses.

3. The End is begun in Moltmann's eschatology by one crucial event, the resurrection of Jesus. Easter is the hinge on which the door of the future swings.

We must ask some questions about this contention:

a. Where are Bethlehem, Galilee and Calvary? Are not these also pieces of history's hinge? The full range of Christ's birth, life, death and resurrection must find a place in eschatology it is to be a responsible reading of the drama of redemption.[10] While the resurrection is the climax of the work of Christ, and the spark that ignited the early Christian community, its significance comes clear only against the backdrop of the full career of Jesus. And there are factors in that pilgrimage that have an integrity of their own easily obscured by the narrowing of the eschatological base to the resurrection.

We have made use of the 'second Adam' framework as a way to lift up the partnership of the life and death of Christ with the resurrection in the healing of history. His message of the coming of the Kingdom, his temptations, his healings and confrontations with men and nature, his death and his resurrection represent contests with the powers in which the control of man's future is wrested from them. And this human activity is seen as the gracious work of an incarnate Love. Resurrection is the copestone of the eschatological arch in its conquest of the 'last enemy', but there are other building blocks.

b. Intimately related to Moltmann's stress upon the resurrection is his assessment of the importance of the fact of death in human life.

> All utopias of the kingdom of God or man, all hopeful pictures of the happy life, all revolutions of the future, remain hanging in the air and bear within them the germ of boredom and decay—and for that reason also adopt a militant and extortionate attitude to life—as long as there is no certainty in the face of death, and no hope carries love beyond death.[11]

While Moltmann makes a searching critique of existentialist preoccupation with internal quandaries about the meaninglessness of life, it is apparent that at this point existentialist anxieties have made their appearance in his own eschatology. To grant to the question of death the controlling role here acknowledged by Moltmann, psychologically and ontologically, does not do justice to some important post-existentialist developments in both modern history and modern thought. The latter come under the broad umbrella of *secularization*.

Secularization does its work in the modern psyche when new generations increasingly free of a life that is nasty, brutish and short begin to taste the exhilaration of human possibilities rather than the anguish of its impossibilities. The focus of men in societies shaped by science-technology is increasingly towards new vistas out and ahead as represented by the futurological inquiries cited earlier. The same process of secularization under the influence of the empirical posture of science-technology tends to be *ad hoc*, issue-oriented and pragmatic. The centre of gravity of this move does not seem to be boredom or despair over the long-range prospects of a death that would extinguish the meaning of their personal or historical projects. Men fix upon the task of finding solutions to problems that confront them and do not ask the 'big key' questions about ultimate destination. Whether this is right or wrong is not the question we focus on here. The point is, an eschatology that lifts up the resurrection as the basic theme of interpretation to a generation presumed to be struggling with the problem of finitude may be giving answers to questions that are not being asked. It may also be that Moltmann's running debate with Bloch has bent his own reflection in this direction, for the 'big key' tendencies of an older, more ideologically oriented Marxism are to be found in the latter's thinking. In any case, to the extent that Moltmann assumes a point of contact with man's anxiety over death, the influence of existential motifs deflect him from a conversation with a more outward-looking, pragmatic era.

There is another aspect of secularization which raises further questions about the death–resurrection forum into which much of Moltmann's eschatology is cast. Here we tread on very uncertain ground. But to take future-orientation seriously we must be willing to cross new borders and step on untested terrain. Can God's action in raising the dead be as compelling a Christian theme as it was in former times, when man himself is now beginning to walk and work in terms of developments that have the smell of that future which for so long was assumed to be alone a divine prerogative? We enter an awesome era of new human capability. Organ transplant, revival of heart-beat, plans not altogether of a science-fiction character for the freezing and resuscitation of both the quick and the dead, and other startling innovations, all point to human control of life that must surely make us stop and think about traditional resurrection theories. In fact, there is increasing perplexity about the line between life and death itself, as witness recent debates on the morality of organ removal.

To root eschatology in the claim that here in Christ's revival is the one place where death is transcended, done by the divine act which exposes human frailty and overcomes its finitude, is a shaky interpretative platform in an ageric age. But worse, it is the example of a *deus ex machina* theology which is neither alert to the powers of men come of age, nor capable of grasping the divine grace at work at men's strong points, the resurrecting grace that manifests itself in man's capacity to confront and ultimately overcome the enigma of his existence. What is needed is an eschatology that sees Christ's own resurrection as the overcoming of the more fundamental death, separation from God. Further it is the breaking down of the doors of physical death and thus the opening of the way for man to follow suit. He is the first of a new race who pioneered, showing men the way to follow. And as God was in Christ in this *avant-garde* action, so he is in the ingenuity and creativity of man as he seeks to shape the future that Christ has opened for him, even the future of death.

4. The Deus ex Machina

We have touched on the elements of a God-of-the-gaps theology that appears in Moltmann's theses on the resurrection. This posture characterizes his eschatology in general. He sees modern alternatives to the Christian hope as destructive to man and his history. Thus those moods and philosophies prone to 'acedia' withdraw men from the historical drama imperilling both the despairer and his society. And the alternative posture towards the future, a 'presumption' which naïvely believes that man can manage his own destiny, is finally shattered on the rock of the facts of evil or breeds a destructive arrogance. Also, it drives man towards the quest for and a temptation to cling to a historical kernel, which option leads to the stagnation of history. It is only by the Christian hope that history can be kept alive by flashes from the future, and led to continually renew itself as it presses towards the End.

The Christian hoper, we most firmly believe, has a mission to perform and a gift to share. Hope's understanding of the powers of evil, future-orientation and whetted expectations, and its belief in the freedom of man to change his own future are things that secular ears need to hear. But in the final analysis, these insights of faith can be secularized. Already they have been to some extent, in some of the modern hopers we have considered. And that fact is cause for joy. God wants a man to be a man. He wants us to face our own problems in the maturity he gives us in these coming-of-age times of accelerated capability to control the environment. To be a man is to seize one's own future. It is the refusal to let the fates or furies, the philosophies or theologies of man beguile us from taking that responsibility. Therefore, whatever contribution faith makes to man's future, it does so within the rhythm of a pioneering-relinquishing stance, pinpointing neglected truths and encouraging man to verify them for himself, then stepping aside so that man can do his work as man.

Christian hope does not have any wisdom about human perplexities that man cannot in principle discover for himself. But it does know about another dimension of the future that is not caught in the net of man's problem-solving. It speaks about One who comes tomorrow and Tomorrow. He calls out to us to company with him in confession, thanksgiving, resolve, adoration and action. He invites us to discover him in and through the solving of our problems – not as the One who is honoured because he can do things we can't, but rather as the One who makes himself known in our own very efforts to humanize the future. When we seek him as an item on the agenda of our felt need, he eludes us. But when he is sought for his own sake, the prayer for his coming is answered.

(ii) Pierre Teilhard de Chardin

'I swore to myself on the body of my dead friend, to fight more vigorously than ever to give hope to man's work and enquiry.'[12] Teilhard kept his vow. The exploration of the grounds of promise is a dominant motif in his intellectual pilgrimage. Towards the end of his life he compared his quest to that of a group of trapped miners struggling upward towards release. To sight light at the end of the tunnel brings rebirth to their spirits and generates the determination to press on to freedom. So also the human race needs to see an 'issue', a way out, if it is to muster the will to move forward. If men believe that a futile history or a burnt-out universe (entropy) awaits them out ahead, such despair will be self-fulfilling prophecy. Could the two worlds in which he participated as palaeontologist and priest – science and religion – yield up any evidence for light at the end of the temporal tunnel? He devoted his life to answering that question.

Interlaced with Teilhard's grapple with the hope was another concern that grew out of his dual existence as a man of science and a man of faith. He was sensitive to the tendency of many both within and without the Christian community to polarize the earthly and heavenly vocations. Must religious belief compete with the investigation and ennoblement of this world? Could the man of faith not express his love for God in the very act of 'building the earth'? And was it not possible that the one ingredient needed for man to accomplish his mission was the witness of the Christian faith?

To 'give hope to man's work', and to encourage in that enterprise the mutual fructification of reason and faith, Teilhard brought the tools of his scientific experience and his Christian commitments. We shall trace the outlines of the structure he crafted towards the future, using these two instruments. We look first at his phenomenologically rooted analysis of a developing world and then to the Christian vision which crowns and completed his data and conjectures.

Cosmogenesis

Genèse – that is the key that unlocks the universe. The cosmos is no static given; it becomes. Within the process there is to be discerned the 'law of complexification and consciousness'. Running from pre-life, through life, to human life is to be found a unitive movement that leads each stage of organization to greater levels of complexity and inter-relationship. And with that integrative growth comes the heightening of a quality latent in the most elemental stuff of the universe, consciousness. While only in the human phenomenon has consciousness attained 'reflective thought', there is no nook or cranny of space-time that is devoid of a 'within'. 'Hominization' is the coming of man, the leap forward of the cosmic process through the 'radial energy' which all along the line had been the catalyst of an enlarging range of 'withinness' (while 'tangential energy' has done its companion work of complexifying the network of 'withoutness'). At this stage of 'cosmogenesis' (the name for the total movement of *genèse* the 'noosphere' appears, a globe-encircling 'membrane' or envelope of thought that distinguishes the phenomenon of man from the biosphere out of whose loins it was born.

Genèse, the impulse towards the future which works according to the law of complexity-consciousness, meets a new kind of challenge in the noosphere. Complexification continues apace as the mobility of the race, the round habitat of the earth, expanding knowledge and ultimately accelerating science-technology combine to draw mankind together in tighter interdependencies. However, there is nothing inevitable, at this stage, in the cosmogenic process. Man, with his character of self-determination, can decide his own future. He is given the freedom to co-operate in the press towards unity. He can see before him, by extrapolation, the goal of *genèse*, the 'Omega Point'. He can make out a movement in the noosphere which stretches towards a new unity in which mankind itself comes to self-consciousness. That is, the envelope of thought reaches such an intense 'temperature' that the long-sought final unity, the 'issue', the end of the tunnel, is reached. That such a possibility suggested by the present momentum in the noosphere will in fact happen is, from a human point of view, still only conjecture. Man could abuse his freedom to build, and instead destroy.

We have sketched thus far Teilhard's 'hyperphysics', speculation about the direction and destiny of the cosmos, but based upon the data of the sciences. By this kind of disciplined imagination Teilhard brings men to the borders of the land of hope.

Within the boundaries of this same disciplined imagination but hinting at something more is Teilhard's effort to demonstrate the reasonableness of a ground and goal of cosmogenesis, a

'Centre' which bears and leads it towards completion: Either the whole construction of the world presented here is vain ideology or, somewhere around us, in one form or another, some excess of personal, extra-human energy should be perceptible to us if we look carefully, and should reveal to us the great Presence.[13]

The whetted appetite for the future stirred by a phenomenological analysis of the universe and the logic of a divine Centre press towards a completion that spills out of the structures of human thought. It cannot remain conjecture. The need to know that there will be light at the end of the tunnel is a yearning planted by God himself, and he alone can satisfy it. This he does by his own self-disclosure. Revelation crowns the struggles of reason, grace completes nature. Teilhard turns our eyes to the Light that is strong enough to pierce the darkness.

Christogenesis

Although the term did not appear until the later years of Teilhard's intellectual journey, the accents of Christogenesis were from the beginning fundamental parts of his vision of the universe. Thus the convergence of things towards their fulfilment is always seen as the work of the drawing power of 'Christ-Omega'. Seen from the perspective of its end, the *genèse* of the cosmos is the *genèse* of Christ. Key elements in Christic development are incarnation, crucifixion, resurrection and parousia. Filling out the drama are Teilhard's conceptions of creation as the work of Christ, and his understanding of the Church and the Eucharist.

Christogenesis touches down in the noosphere at Bethlehem. Incarnation happens so that the divine may 'take control' of the processes of complexification and consciousness from within their theatre of action. The divine identification includes solidarity with the suffering and death that overshadow the forward movement. Yet bearing the burden of evil that is inseparable from growth, Christ is raised, thus signalling that death is a metamorphosis into higher reaches of spirit and is no longer a threat to the fulfilment of the universe. In the resurrection, God secures the outcome; Omega will be.

The glorified humanity of Christ, a 'physically' present Body, continues the unitive surge through the Church. Sometimes Teilhard expresses the meaning of the Church as a 'phylum of love' set in the human flow in order to lead it to the final togetherness which only such love can achieve. At other times he lifts up the Eucharist as the axis through which Incarnate Word radiates his presence and power in the universe, a 'prolongation of transubstantiation' in which the universe blazes with the divine Fire. However expressed, Teilhard sees the cosmos, diaphanous with his glory, undergoing a Christification that drives towards the 'Omega Point'.

Before examining the concept of Omega from the angle of revelation, note should be taken of Teilhard's extension of Christogenesis towards the beginning as well as the end. Adapting the classic idea that Christ is present and at work in the origin of the world, Teilhard builds into his own vision a picture of Christ in his full Personhood as the active agent from the beginning of the evolutionary thrust. He is Alpha and Omega. While the direct Christogenic action takes place on the stage of the noosphere, it also goes on from the inception of cosmic integration.

A good deal of confusion surrounds the notion of the 'Omega Point', as the concept is used in different contexts by Teilhard. Read from below, as the issue of cosmogenesis, the Omega Point takes on the characteristics of a new historical emergent, mankind coming to self-consciousness, the flowing together of the noosphere in such a fashion that it brings to final flower the seeds of withinness in evolution. Viewed 'from above', in the light of Christian faith, what appeared to the eyes of reason as a natural development takes on the lustre of Parousia, the 'return of Christ', which opens the way for the fulfilment of the Pauline vision in which God is all in all. Teilhard holds that as the phylum of love approaches the culmination of its work in perfecting the human form, encouraging the press towards knowledge and research, the zeal to build the earth, and weaving a web of love that binds persons in community without sacrificing their dignity, the Christ-Omega bursts through the fabric of time to bring fulfilment. The final convergence of the Christic and the cosmic processes marks the end of time. While it is Christ who initiates the future's finale, it is nevertheless true that the ground must first be prepared for his second Advent. Thus the cultivation of the final fruit by man is the 'necessary although not sufficient' condition of its ripening. Consonant with orthodox portrayals of the End, Teilhard sees as a strong possibility that not all will participate in the fulfilment, as remnants of evil continue to seek to retard the cosmic progression. The ecstatic shattering of time as it confronts the One who comes will be marked by the breaking loose of the loving fragment drawn towards the new day of life with God while the destructive element goes to its death.

In Teilhard's words the Omega-Point is described:

One day, the Gospel tells us, the tension gradually accumulating between humanity and God will touch the limits prescribed by the possibilities of the world. And then will come the end. Then the presence of Christ, which has been silently accruing in things, will suddenly be revealed—like a flash of light from pole to pole. Breaking through all the barriers within which the veil of matter and the water-tightness of souls have seemingly kept it confined, it will invade the face of the earth. . . . Like lightning, like a conflagration, like a flood, the attraction exerted by the Son of Man will lay hold of all the whirling elements in the universe so as to reunite them or subject them to his body. . . . Such will be the consummation of the divine *milieu*.[14]

Agreements and Disagreements

As in the case of Moltmann, we shall not attempt a detailed assessment of Teilhard's eschatology, but rather explore points of harmony and dissonance with the themes developed in Chapter 2. We follow the design of hope set forth earlier in making the comparison.

The very question that dominates Teilhard's work is a recognition of the plight in which man and the world find themselves, despair of entrapment in a tunnel with no exit. There is no naïve glossing over of the forces ranged against the cosmic enterprise: suffering as a constant in the universal convergence, sin as a possibility that will in fact deter a section of humanity from sharing in fulfilments of the Omega Point, and a death which from a human point of view – and in the believer, in his all-too-human moments – casts a shadow over the personal and cosmic future. These themes disqualify any interpretation of Teilhard that dismisses his point of view as a simple optimism.

Ernst Benz has said that Teilhard is one of the powerful voices in modern thought that have taught men how to hope again. Thus, in the midst of his awareness of evil, Teilhard refuses to acknowledge its power over the future. He directs our gaze beyond the bleakness of the moment to the tunnel opening. His influence today is related not only to the future-oriented character of his thought, but also to its hopefulness. And he has explored with rare sensitivity and depth the eschatological themes of the Christian faith in an attempt to move the conversation with the secular hopers and the secular despairers forward.

A particular contribution he makes to Christian futurology is his accent on the cosmic setting of hope. Not only does he provide a forum for dialogue between the science community and the faith community, but he breaks out of personal and historical categories to which theology regularly limits the range of divine action. Nature too is drawn into the eschatological drama.

While pointed clearly to the 'Not Yet', Teilhard's expectation theology does not succumb to a futuristic reductionism. The God who waits for us out ahead is also vigorously at work in the 'Now'. His presence, as well as his promise, confronts us in the divine milieu that animates nature and history and comes to expression in the life of the Church.

With a searching understanding of the springs of human behaviour, he also knows that present evidence for fulfilment yet to be must include the knowledge that man has some influence over that future:

> We shall never bend our backs to the task that has been allotted us of pushing noogenesis onwards except on condition that the effort demanded of us has a chance of succeeding and of taking us as far as possible. . . . Man will never take a step in a direction he knows to be blocked.[15]

His struggle to accord to man this freedom for the future can be seen in his description of the challenge of the noospheric level of cosmogenesis. He asserts that its evolutionary singularity lies in man's capacity to determine the outcome of the process. Men can make or break the march forward according to their response to its claim. Whether he can maintain this great theme throughout his vision we shall presently examine, but its accents can certainly be heard frequently in his writings.

Action is the child of Teilhardian future-orientation. In fact it is 'the problem of action' that underlies his definition of the human plight – how man can be saved from an enervating despair and be moved to seize his destiny. While action is often interpreted to mean the pursuit and implementation of a knowledge that expands man's noospheric status, intertwined with it is a love that unites and ennobles. Thus hope propels into mission, the Church, serving as the phylum of love, drawing men towards the fulfilment of the process of creative integration.

While each of the joints in our skeletal structure of Christian hope show similarities with Teilhard's eschatology, there are some marked dissimilarities. Here are a few of the salient questions that grow out of the former perspective and must be directed at the Teilhardian theses:

1. How radical is the assessment of the problem of evil? Does Teilhard's attempt to do it justice in his vision reach the full depths of the biblical analysis? The cosmogenic process, however scarred by the powers arrayed against it, does move ineluctably upward towards its goal. The escalator creaks and groans under the weight of its passengers and their destructive antics, but it does grind on towards the End. The phylum of love inserted in history, and the universal grace at work, are irresistible as the ascent is made.

There are at least three factors at work in Teilhard's perspective which tend to disintegrate the provisional realism which tries to make itself heard in some of the sensitivity cited earlier.

a. Teilhard has set his sights on finding 'light at the end of the tunnel'. In this salutary concern to discover grounds for hope which can stir men to action against the many despairing signs he sees around him, the final confidence of faith has been transferred too easily into intramundane terms. The Christian Story does not report a gradual sloughing off of the lethal factors in human and cosmic existence. Nor is it necessary to believe that this is so in order for men to be hopeful and to struggle meaningfully for a better tomorrow. Light at the end of the tunnel is needed. But the kind of light that faith makes possible down the penultimate passageways is the assurance that the powers of evil do not control the future. While human effort will not be guaranteed fulfilment, and certainly not so by evolutionary progression of its efforts, it is given the possibility of marching ahead. Faith also sees a final light in its vision of ultimate *shalom*. But it does not insist that men need such second sight in order to hope and to work for a better world. Such hope is an overbelief that does not fight its way into the apologetic arena claiming that life is meaningless without its assurances. It is there as a vision whose only power is its truth for the eyes of faith.

b. Teilhard does his theological work within a Catholic tradition which has often been vulnerable to the temptation of claiming too much for the possibilities of history. Whether it assumes the capacities of men for natural law or natural justice without the serious impingement of sin, or reads the Christian life in semi-Pelagian terms or views the Church too uncritically as an unimpeded expression of divine life, it tends not to measure the retrogressive tendencies deeply enough. These more optimistic estimates are at work in the cosmogenic-Christogenic movement charted by Teilhard, as the natural forward-moving vitalities are crowned and completed by the gracious Christic action that leads the cosmos towards fulfilment. Whereas the forensic theme in Moltmann strips history of living possibilities, over-ambitious sanctification accents populate it too plentifully and assuredly with achievement.

c. The influence of the organic image borrowed from the sciences contributes to the onward and upward flavour of Teilhard's eschatology. Thus 'growth', entirely appropriate in a description of natural processes, comes to mean at the level of history the progression towards moral maturity with the same inevitability as a seed coming to flower.

2. A second serious problem in Teilhard's eschatology, closely related to the absence of radical sobriety about the human and cosmic venture, has to do with the sealing off of

the future. To affirm that faith assures the direction and completion of a cosmic process is to put a question mark over the effective freedom of man to control his own destiny. In so far as the terrestrial future is directed, and its outcome is guaranteed by, divine favour, that future is predetermined. As such, it is not within the power of man really to control it. There is a 'big Daddy' that presides over it, no matter how benevolent his intentions. This historical triumphalism does not do justice to the biblical thesis we have sought here to defend, that man is given the right to be man, to manage his own future, for better or for worse. Moreover, if we are right in our analysis of the components of human hoping, it does not do justice to a very fundamental one of these: the belief that men can affect their future significantly. It is not the assurance that 'everything will come out all right in the end' that generates hope. That may, in fact, breed apathy. Rather it is the belief that it may or may not come out all right in the end, depending on what we do about it right now – and the companion assurance that what we do right now can make a difference – that spurs action.

There are surely indications in Teilhard's writing that suggest this later thesis especially the periodic insistence that at the noospheric level the way ahead is indeed up to man. But the general drift of his thought, especially as it is controlled by the above three considerations, drives it towards the thesis that there is a surge within the cosmos which moves ineluctably towards its destination. That mechanism represents a closure of real human responsibility for what is to be.

3. The 'already' dimension of the eschatological rhythm, as it is worked out by Teilhard in the 'Eucharist and Body of Christ' teachings, bears closer inspection. Again, as within the Catholic tradition, there is a strong tendency to heighten the significance of ecclesiastical phenomena. Thus the divine milieu in which we live is seen as a prolongation

94

of God's churchly action and hence a secondary phenomenon. Apart from the difficulty of seeing how the worldly Christ's presence in some sense depends on the actual
celebrations of the institutional Church, the question must
be asked if the full freedom of Christ to range over his
world is being honoured in these formulations. Is there not
a danger of domesticating Deity by interpreting his sover-
eignty as if it were an emanation of the Church? Is the
Christ at work in the cosmic heights and depths a 'secondary' reality?

Theology and faith must find some way to honour the
full integrity of the work of Christ in both Church and
world. Currently popular 'secular Christologies' in Prote-
stantism are so eager to stress the action of Christ on non-
ecclesiastical terrain that they obscure or distort the biblical
testimony to his presence and work within the Christian
community. On the other hand, traditional opinions
remain enamoured of the Christ – Church bond and find
little or no room for the secular work of Christ. Hence the
polarization between Christ→World→Church and Christ
→Church→World ecclesiologies. Teilhard is to be thanked
for his effort to move beyond these oversimplified options
by attempting to affirm both churchly and extra-churchly
Christic grace. However, in his effort to remain within the
confines of the high ecclesiology of traditional Catholic
teaching, he seems to have tipped the scales markedly on
the churchly side, as the 'axis' of the cosmic Christ's life and
action still passes through the Church, and the Eucharist
specifically.

A clue to finding a way through this dilemma is the
Emmaus Road story. On the road, Christ was fully present
to his disciples, yet incognito. In Emmaus he was also
their companion, but through the 'breaking of bread'
he became known. Are there not two comparable relations

95

that Christ sustains with his world in our own time? He is present as our unannounced companion where *shalom* is at work in history and cosmos, wherever the diseases of war, hate, injustice, poverty are contested by the healing processes and movements of men, wherever the fissures and fractures in nature are drawn together in greater unity. Men truly participate in his life and work when they are party to these reconciling currents. He is their comrade in alongsided pilgrimage ('I–He' relation) towards his goal, even though they – revolutionary, reformer, prophet, pioneer, scientist, philosopher – do not recognize him, do not acknowledge him, do not confess his name. He is there, but incognito.

But he is 'cognito' in the breaking of Bread. Within the faith community where his name is known, his story told, and his presence celebrated, he comes to men in disclosure. In the sacramental meal and in the interpretative Word, he makes himself known as he did at Emmaus. Here men find him in the I–Thou encounter of confession, thanksgiving, adoration.

Because it is the one Christ with whom we have to do, these confrontations on the road and at the meal are torn apart only at our peril. The incognito Christ is served with fullness only when men know who it is that they company with in their pilgrimage of *shalom*. That is the purpose of Christian Story-telling, evangelism as *kerygma*. The One who is alongside us 'in profile' seeks to meet us in 'eye to eye' disclosure. But those who know him only face to face in the celebrations of the community, and have not travelled with him over the laborious and dangerous roads of worldly service, can only meet a sorrowing, yes, and an angry Lord who declares, 'Depart from me, you cursed, into the eternal fire prepared for the devil and his angels; for I was hungry and you gave me no food, I was thirsty and you gave me no drink, I was a stranger and you did not welcome me, naked and you did not clothe me, sick and in prison and you did not visit me . . . as you did it not to one of the least of these, you did it not to me' (Matthew 25: 41–45).

4. While we can be grateful to Teilhard for bringing the world of nature and the whole cosmos into the eschatological processes, and thus pressing Christian thought beyond the arena of human history by which much contemporary theology is mesmerized, it is also true that the historical receives less than the attention which is its due. Specifically, the political, social and economic dimensions of mission nowhere get the commanding significance that belongs to them in an era of unprecedented historical ferment. The scale of missionary mandate is laid out in *The Phenomenon of Man* as, first, the increase of knowledge; second, the improvement of the species by eugenic advances; and third, the role of religion. The last includes the ministry of love and could be the jumping-off point for the kind of structure-splitting action that Moltmann sees required by the eschatological vision; but none is forthcoming. It might well be that precisely those eugenic developments, and questions brought about by the explosion of knowledge which Teilhard welcomes, will demand the kind of radical commitment to social, economic, and political issues which is muted in Teilhard's perspective. We shall pursue this point in Chapter 4.

Teilhard de Chardin asks, 'What faith will open tomorrow for us?' His eschatology is a profound and instructive wrestle with this question. Whatever its shortcomings, it has widened the door of the future for Christians, and for that this expectant generation is in his debt.

III Harvey Cox

Since the publication in 1965 of *The Secular City*, Harvey

Cox has become one of the most influential theologians in the Anglo-Saxon world. His recent interest in the theme of hope has contributed significantly to the rejuvenation of eschatology. Cox, as yet, has not worked out his position with the details of a Teilhard de Chardin or a Moltmann, but the lines of its development are beginning to emerge. A recent series of essays, *On Not Leaving it to the Snake*, addresses itelf to the question of the future. We shall base our review of his perspective on these data, calling in other recent writing in the same genre, and some of the theses of *The Secular City* in so far as they are foundational for the more current reflection on Christian futurology.

As there is no clear cut eschatology in Cox's published work as yet, we shall try to ascertain the shape of his thought by looking first at some of the general focuses of theological construction. They are important clues to the direction of his work.[16]

A. *Secularization* is a fundamental motif. We select here four characteristics of the process which, for Cox, is a decisive influence in our era.

1. *This-worldliness*. Urban men in a technological society are preoccupied with the issues of this world and this time. And rightly so, as capabilities for ennobling or destroying the earth have sky-rocketed. If the Christian community is to make its way meaningfully in an empirical era, and serve responsibly in a world where the 'stakes have been raised' in human issues, then it must think, live and minister in secular terms. Commitment to this style means putting a question mark over metaphysical and theological talk of another world alongside this one, and in particular, disengaging Christian faith from the Greek categories which perpetuate this duality.

2. *Maturity*. Inextricably bound up with this-worldliness,

yet a distinguishable feature of secularization, is the 'coming of age' dimension of the process.[17] Man increasingly can do the things he formerly assigned to the gods or to God; and he knows it. Cox wants the Church to affirm man's maturity. No reconceptualization of faith which invites childishness can makes its home in a society which has learned to 'make it' without the symbols, rituals, ideas and institutions of religion.

3. *Pragmatism*. While he is ready to challenge an over-zealous pragmatism, Cox believes faith should find its way into the idiom of the 'little key', the *ad hoc*, the step-by-step procedure that rejects ambitious ideologies, and tests the validity of ideas by their efficacy. It can be expected that the question, 'What opens the future?' will be an important one.

4. *Historicity*. The secularization process tends to relativize perspectives. We are becoming increasingly aware of the 'social location' of idea systems. The importance of this sense of contingency takes different forms in Cox's thinking. (*a*) Inherited beliefs are, by definition, the deposits of another era. In a period of rapid change, the relevance of an inheritance born from another womb is suspect. Can a concept that might have been right for another time fit a new era that is radically different? (*b*) Contemporary thought must be geared to its own historical nexus. (*c*) The work of theology must rise from deep participation in, and ministry to, the human issues of our present history. (*d*) As the urban-technological factors shape our time, theology must do its work self-consciously in relation to, and in immersion in, the secular city.

B. We label the second feeder element in Cox's developing eschatology, the *existential impulse*. This might seem odd in the light of Cox's critique of existentialist

99

preoccupation with meaninglessness, despair, and internal quandaries of decision and quests for identity. However, alongside the attack, there is also an affirmation of a crucial existentialist interest: the appropriation of our humanity by the will to act, and the call to cast away the crutches and contest the tyrannies that impede self-determination. We shall see this theme very much at work in Cox's eschatological reflection.

C. The departure from the conventional wisdom of existentialism is marked by the *political framework* in which the will to act is lived out. Decision is public, corporate, structural, calculated to effect change in the life of the *polis*.

D. Cox's definition of the *theologian's role* affects his eschatological posture. The theologian is related to the Church with particular responsibility for its cutting edge. He serves the 'prophetic community', committed to servanthood in a secular age.

E. *Specific theological themes* that are formative in his eschatology include: (1) the prophetic tradition in the Old Testament, especially its humanizing and future-oriented accents; (2) the ageric notes in the Old Testament which assert man's role as partner in creation; (3) the New Testament portrait of Christ as the 'Man for others' in the Bonhoeffer idiom; (4) the Kingdom of God framework of 'already' – 'not yet', and characterization of it as *'shalom'* showing influences of the World Council of Churches' study of the Missionary Structure of the Congregation; (5) the Church as the *avant-garde* of *shalom*; (6) a reconceptualization of Deity in de-hellenized, futurized terms under the influence of Ernst Bloch, Teilhard de Chardin, Leslie Dewart.

F. Cox's theology is shaped by his *involvement* in today's revolutionary ferment in its various expressions – the struggle for black rights, the peace movement, student revolt, and Marxist–Christian dialogue.

G. Not always given its full due, but none the less of considerable importance is his church existence in the *left-wing Reformation tradition* as an American Baptist. This has meant not only a self-conscious effort to rediscover the revolutionary bite of the left-wing tradition, but is reflected in his criticism of the magisterial reformers, in his conception of the church and in the Anabaptist accents implicit in his stress on man's role in the redemptive processes.

The Contours of a Developing Eschatology

Cox has been occupied recently with the meaning of the Old Testament. We begin our search for the roots of his eschatology there.

With the 'snake' figure Cox takes us to the doors of Israel's history. Talk about the future is launched at the furthest reaches of the past: creation. In the myth of our beginnings Adam and Eve are called by God to 'subdue the earth', to 'name the animal', in short to build a habitable world from the raw materials which the Creator has furnished. The vocation of mankind, therefore is seen to be a stewardship of the earth which brings to fulfilment its possibilities by initiative and imagination. In his earlier formulations, Cox sees this as an invitation by Deity to co-creatorship.

As the story unfolds, mankind's representative figures, Adam and Eve, fail to execute their mandate. Cox sees the role of the serpent as of special significance, for its success in beguiling Eve means that humanity has fled its call to partnership; man has succumbed to the forces of the earth instead of subduing them. In the success of the serpent, that is, in 'leaving it to the snake', a 'source sin' of man makes its appearance: acedia. We have long been prevented from appreciating the centrality of lassitude in man's downfall because an anti-rebellion social and political establishment encouraged the notion that pride is the basic human problem. This ideology must be overthrown by exposing 'the hollow men and carbuncular clerks' whose problem is not 'privateering' but the retreat to passivity before the modern challenges that demand ardour and revolutionary action.

It became the portion of the prophets to recall the Covenant people, and through them the world, to take the task which mankind had abdicated. Prophetic future-orientation turned the face of Israel forward, calling it towards a remade world in which wolf and lamb, men and nations were reconciled, and warning it that it would suffer the consequences of disobedience. What happened would depend on the moral effort put forth then and there by the Jew in response to the vision. That is, the prophet did not approach the future as a soothsayer deciphering a puzzle. His interest in what was to come was related to his effort to stir the chosen people to penitent and healing action in the immediacies of their history.

Prophetic futurity is to be contrasted with teleological and apocalyptic eschatologies. Teleology treats tomorrow as the exfoliation of a development latent in the seeds of its origin. It thus punctures any hope that men can control their future one way or the other, for the outcome is predetermined. Apocalypse is engrossed in an End that is outside the boundaries of time, and thus also beguiles man from the task of building the earth. It is only in prophetism that men are encouraged to seize the reins of their own history, for the future is viewed as an open one, whose outcome could be disastrous or redemptive according to the responses they make to their mandate.

With the coming of Jesus, the prophetic line is re-asserted but with a difference. Whatever parochialism attended Israel's picture of the future is abolished, for here is forecast a universal *shalom*, into which Gentile as well as Jew are welcomed. But more, something new is introduced, a new vision. Here is a 'new Adam' not beguiled by the snake, but one who shoulders the task of making a habitable earth in venturing responsibility. In his life of active *shalom* he embodies the Kingdom envisaged as the goal of creation, and points to the signs of its inbreaking.

From this central Happening of the future is born a community of memory and hope. The church looks back to the Herald and his prophetic ancestry, and forward to the Kingdom of promise. It bears witness to the 'already – not yet' tension in which it lives by *avant-garde* action for freedom, justice and peace, the struggle to make real *shalom* in its own life, and identifying and celebrating the signs of reconciliation in its testimony (*diakonia, koinonia, kerygma*).

It is interesting that this scenario can be laid out with almost no explicit reference to Deity. 'God', in Cox's view, has been abused by association with cultural values, and has alienated a secular society by affiliation with an outworn metaphysics. Further, 'post-literature' man responds to visibilities – and thus to what the Church does rather than to what it says. These factors propel us towards modesty in God-talk. But they do not eliminate the question as to whether we are 'alone in the universe'. Cox remains committed to the reality of an Other, and is uneasy both with alternatives that use the label 'God' for immanent processes or dimensions that can be described by others in secular terms, and also with Christian atheism. He is trying to be faithful to a secular sensitivity which has no time for Platonic supra-worlds, and thus demands a 'no-nonsense "levelling" in theological discourse', yet wants to do justice in this theology to a Reality which Christian faith has asserted as standing outside of our processes, saving us from closure and idolatry. He thus 'edges cautiously' towards new formulations that do take into account both concerns, acknowledging that the way is uncertain and the traps many.

Along this catwalk towards future formulations about God, Cox is helped by Teilhard and Ernst Bloch. Showing the influence of the 'Omega Point' idea and Bloch's reconceptualization of God as the historical 'Not Yet', Cox experiments with the idea of substituting 'will be' for 'is' in describing the divine action. One non-empirical dimension of reality which a secular age does take seriously is the future. This is particularly true of the visionary and revolutionary in the Marxist and left-wing Reformation traditions whose commitment to the reality of the future evokes radical action. He sees the need for going beyond Bloch's limiting 'God' to future historical possibilities, as this opens the door for uncritical absolutizing of a sector of finitude with its attendant dangers of fanaticism and utopianism. Cox seeks to preserve the distance between history and the Other in some sense out ahead of it and never identifiable with any particular social configuration. He also finds helpful Leslie Dewart's proposal to talk in terms of God's 'presence' as the 'pressure of the future', rather than of the 'existence of God'.

Out of these varied influences as they are filtered through a mesh made up of the threads of thought earlier examined, a concept of God begins to emerge in which 'the One who comes' takes the place of 'He who is'. From out ahead of us in time he comes towards us, drawing all men to him, upsetting the securities in which we barricade ourselves against the future, and calling for a venturing faith into the 'Not Yet'.

Response: Sin and God

Cox's eschatology and the structure of hope we are developing in these pages have many affinities. The Old and New Testament vision of *shalom* is seen as the goal of redemption, and Jesus is viewed as the point of its entry and his career as the arena in which the Man for others demonstrates the meaning of the responsible life to a mankind trapped in its inability to act towards the future. Cox comes down especially hard on the note of man's freedom to shape his own future, holding that the outcome of the historical venture is truly left in human hands. He interprets God as supportive of the human pilgrimage in calling us out of our present and towards his future. There are, however, some fundamental differences. We focus on two.

Sin

Cox asserts that acedia is the most dangerous expression of sin. Is this true? It may indeed be correct that the most virulent form of human incurvature in some historical and sociological contexts is apathy. For example, if we are confronting an institutional Church with significant resources for the struggle against blatant evil, yet loth to become involved, then prophetic diatribe against sloth is well placed. If the opening chapter in *On Not Leaving it to the Snake* on the serpentine temptation to abdicate from involvement were a sermon in ecclesiastical setting it would ring true.*

---

* But how appropriate is this homily in the face of this testimony about the prisoners of Treblinka? 'It was not despair that they felt, but a kind of lethargy, an immense lassitude in the heart of this interminable continental winter, under the blows, with hunger in their bellies, in this world of death, at the mercy of this implacable machine which exterminated with frightening regularity' (Steiner *Treblinka* p. 184). Accusations of lethargy slide so easily into a moralism that ignores the creaturely rootage of man, and thus a misunderstanding of man as a

105

But let us assume that this interpretation of sin lays claim to general relevance for our time, as it appears to do. We must then test it in other settings that characterize our era. How would this exhortation and its corollary, the rejection of 'pride' as the root sin in a day when it is not Promethean defiance but the temptation 'to weasel out' that constitutes our main problem, fit in the midst of the needs of the communities and movements that are most formative of our present and our future? Is it lassitude against which the Church must give warning in its conversation with the scientist, doctor, political leader, and industrialist who discover and make operational the explosion of new instruments of man's power over life? Must the young, the black, and the poor who now surge forward to claim their humanity be given counsel by Christians on the dangers of non-involvement? While there are many who do not share their brothers' revolutions, the pacesetters in our time, those who form the new ethos, are the ageric. Sloth is not their problem.

The testimony that faith has to bring to modern men at these bursting centres of new power and life (and it must be from within the life of these movements that Christian dialogue proceeds) is a celebration of struggle to seize their future, blended with an astringent realism about the possibilities of a new megalomania, as|disastrous as that of the autocrats whose bondage they throw off. The temptations of pride are not confined to a period in which Reinhold Niebuhr warned of totalitarian Babel-builders. They are very much with us in any era in which men are caught up in the rush of new power. That is particularly true of our world as it flexes its muscles in coming of age. As Bonhoeffer noted in some thoughtful commentary on the culpabilities of

disembodied angel rather than as one who lives 'at the juncture of nature and spirit'.

modern men, 'It is not the sins of weakness, but the sins of strength which matter here.'[18]

Cox's stress upon sin as sloth shows the influence of his political and action-oriented predispositions. In fact, a case could be made that Cox's eschatological formulation bears a left-wing Reformation stamp in the same way that Moltmann's perspective is bent in a predominantly Lutheran direction and Teilhard's is shaped along Roman Catholic lines. All honour to the contribution that each tradition can bring to our search for fresh understanding of Christian promise. But historically fragmentary insights imported into modern eschatology distort here as they do in earlier controversies around other doctrines. Cox's dismissal of post-Constantinian Christianity and the magisterial Reformation's understanding of the 'prideful' character of sin as the ideology of state-based religious Establishments which could not tolerate 'insubordination' has enough truth in it to make good tract material for the radical Reformation. However, it obscures more than it illuminates the plight of man and the mission of the Church to an age that must hear somewhere of the vulnerability of its new powers.

Attending the accent on sloth as the critical sin, is a weakening of the problem of sin itself. As a theme of a magisterial Reformation which in some of its major expressions was not notorious for its sense of political mission or revolutionary fervour, sin could be expected not to bulk as large in a Cox eschatology reacting against this wing. His critics have commented on this tendency in *The Secular City*, and it continues in his developing eschatological thought. It is reflected also in the virtual absence of the theme of divine forgiveness. Thus, important dimensions of man's plight and its overcoming are left out in this accounting.

As an alternative to the Cox perspective, there is another

reading of the human situation that also affirms the threat of acedia, but sees it against a larger background of fracture. Drawing on the line of thought that rises from Augustine, and passes through Kierkegaard and Reinhold Niebuhr, the human problem is gauged at the level of the disruption between man and God. Sin is the self's turning away from God and his design for the world towards the patronizing of the self and its interests. In this sense, pride is the fundamental human problem, for man sets himself above the concerns of God and neighbour. Privateering *is* the originative sin. But the forms in which it expresses itself take shape according to the duality of man's location 'at the juncture of nature and spirit'. Man expresses his self-love by erecting some aspect of finitude of his own making or composition (race, class, system, business, nation, party, movement, book, etc.) in the place of love for God, and thus falls prey to more aggressive sin (of the spirit), idolatry sometimes described as pride, although the term might better be reserved for the anterior rift. Self-love, however, might express itself not in heaven-storming, but in passivity. This is the sin of flight. It is the abdication of the responsible life, sinking into forgetfulness by the many tricks men devise for escape, from the sins of the body to the busy whirl of bourgeois existence. Flight may take shape as concupiscence. Or it might form itself into lassitude.

What mask sin wears does change according to the circumstances. Cox is right that, where apathy threatens, the sense of the peril of acedia must be recovered, but so as neither to cripple faith in those contexts in which the right word is counsel about the heaven-storming pretensions of the powerful, nor to obscure the omnipresent root sin of a prideful will which puts its own goal before the goal of *shalom*.[19]

God

The experimental and tentative character of Cox's eschatology is particularly prominent when he deals with the idea of God. In fairness to Cox, we shall treat his proposals as exploratory movements rather than firm commitments, and thus in the spirit of laboratory testing rather than as a call to the colours, pro or con. We shall raise two questions about Cox's provisional formulations about God: Can they be squared with fundamental themes in Christian faith? Are they understandings of God which enable the faith community to affirm secularization in the way Cox himself urges? Both these questions are within the framework of Cox's own commitments, so they should provide a common forum.

The work of God ranges well beyond the radar screen of human subjectivity. God is not contained in or controlled by man's awarenesses of the divine action. Cox has frequently stressed this incognito work of Christ in the world in the humanizing movements of our time. A similar note is struck in his criticism of William Hamilton's version of radical theology. He sees Hamilton taking too hasty a step from his own experiences and feelings to cosmic judgement.

In the light of these observations on the freedom of God from the psychic apparatus of man, a question must be asked about the notion that God may have to be reconceived as a 'pressure' from the future, and about the allied idea that we may have to speak of God as 'present' rather than as 'existing'. This theme seems to be a developing amalgam of some Dewart and Bloch theses. They take shape as the suggestion that God, who cannot be said to exist in the 'Now', is nevertheless with us as a gentle pressure from the future; when this pressure is felt is in the act of a fruitful hoping. The presence of God is the power of a hope that sends men into political action. Where hoping is productive of humanizing, there the divine is at work. The flowing of value from belief (the pragmatic factor in Cox's general orientation) points to a correspondence between belief and an objective structure. Hoping that is ethically fertile argues for the reality of the 'One who comes'.

An assumption that underlies this line of argument is that God's 'presence', and hence whatever reality he has in the 'Now' is hooked to human subjectivity. Where this kind of action-producing hoping goes on – and that would include the secular hopers as well as action-oriented religious visionaries – there God is at work. Where there is no creative hoping, there is no pressure from the future. By the logic of the argument the conclusion must therefore be that God is absent at these places.

There is a nest of problems here: (1) The God of the Christian Story is not tabernacled in human consciousness or action. Surely he may work through it, but he is not domesticated by it. A big God may be present incognito in the process that transcends human knowing, for he ranges over the heights and depths of creation. (2) His orbit extends as well beyond the circumference of human life. To tie his action to the conscious act of hoping does not do justice to the divine creativity present in the natural processes, the structures of society and other sub-ideational (or supra-ideational) dimensions of reality. (3) Is God not to be found among the hopeless? The biblical testimony is that even when we descend to the depths, he is there. Again, formulations that speak of his presence in terms of a pressure in future-oriented action are too narrow to encompass a lively presence shared with those who despair as well as those who hope.

The common note sounded in these questions is the freedom of God, as it refuses to be bound by the psychic activity of man. But there is another implication of this freedom. A truly free God is no more captive to a dimension of time than he is to a sector of space. Eschatological theology is discovering the vista of the future which had been lost from view by dogmas that sought to imprison God in the past or the present. The risk involved in this new discovery is that what is fresh and rightly to the foreground may seek to establish a new monopoly. The Cox declaration that 'if theology can leave behind the God who "is" and begin its work with the God who "will be" . . ., an exciting new epoch in theology could begin . . .,'[20] mixes together a genuine set of new marching orders – the accent on the One who comes – with an invitation to a new captivity. The One who comes is also free to *be*. He roves over the landscape of present and past as well as future.

The crucial issue raised by the relation of God to the theatres of time and space, therefore, is his capacity for self-direction. Is God free to be God in the Cox scenario? Is he free to be Alpha as well as Omega? Anything less than a God who ranges over today and yesterday as well as tomorrow, and is found not only in men's hoping but in 'the uttermost parts of the earth', is less than the biblical God.

A fundamental factor in Cox's hesitation to declare for the full range of divine action is his commitment to the secular city. He does not want to violate a modern mind that has rejected the 'supraterrestrial' dimension, and 'two-storey dualism'. Further, he believes that the focus on a network of transcendent relationships with their source in the God who 'is' has served to divert men's energies from the task of building their earth, and has made them accommodate too easily to oppressive conditions which demand radical change. Thus he seeks to preserve the overagainstness that 'keeps history open' in the biblical conception of God by interpreting it in 'ahead' rather than 'now' categories.

Aheadness calls into question existing conditions, allies God with the forward-moving elements in history, and does not make claims to the 'existence' of a reality that can be dismissed as superstition by an empirical generation.

Let us consider the assumption in this. Cannot a revolutionary impulse arise within a commitment to the God who is here? There is a good deal of evidence from Christian history – running from the New Testament community's transvaluation of its society's values through the left wing of the Reformation to the 19th-century social gospel movements, to today's Church involvements in the modern struggles for justice and freedom – that a belief in the present reality of God does not impede Christians from overturning tables any more than it did the first Revolutionary. It is not the conviction about the existence of God that cripples secular mission, but misunderstanding about the character of the God who exists, the failure to see that his contemporary action does indeed drive towards the future.

In the sound instinct that is suspicious of theological ideas that enable men to nestle into the *status quo* with a good conscience, there is also frequently found a more suspect companion impulse. Traces of it are found in Cox's eschatology. It is the uncritical identification of what is faithful with what is new and different. The demonic has many a ploy. He may appear as the counsel for the defence of the *status quo*. Or he may come wearing the neutral shades of 'the middle way'. And he can make the scene in the flaming colours of the reflex radical. The corruption of responsible radicalism is its institutionalizing. Faith is distorted when it blesses any establishment, be it conservative, middle of the road, or radical. As Christ is free, so is faith. It bows the knee to no one. It has no built-in reflex that always turns tables, or always sets them up. It is enough in control of its own life to let facts, not mechanisms, decide the course of action that will honour or overthrow the givens as the evidence requires. The final test of eschatological action is not its alignment with a human predilection or passion, but its consonance with the Christian Story.

Another assumption that appears to press Cox away from the 'God who is' to the 'God who will be' is the secular restiveness and/or disinterest in 'supraterrestrial' reality. What impairs communication with a this-worldly time is the Greek metaphysical mould in which we have cast our Christian commitments. A de-hellenization is needed which will cleanse our talk of concurrent invisible worlds, but will still make room for the kind of non-empirical reality to which creative and revolutionary moderns resonate, the future.

We believe that Cox is right in locating the centre of divine gravity in the future. Eschatology is the medium through which faith is most meaningfully stated for a secular and future-oriented time. However, in Christian dialogue with contemporaries, there is a crucial line that must be respected; the boundary between communication and accommodation. It is crossed when we begin to say the same things our era says, except in a louder voice, and in more picturesque language. It is crossed when embarrassing, awkward and uninteresting notes in our orchestration get muted because they are offensive to modern ears. The developing Cox eschatology must answer the inquiry as to how it is not moving in this direction in its adaptation to secular sensibilities.

De-hellenization is indeed a crucial aspect of up-dating theology. But as I have argued elsewhere, it does not include the excision of the present transcendence of God any more than an eminently non-Platonic Hebrew prophetism

113

censored the concurrent 'behind the scenes' presence of Yahweh in the great historical dramas of their time.[21]

Will secular men tune us out if we continue to speak of a present Other as well as the One who will be? Perhaps so. It would not be the first time Christian faith proved to be a stumbling block to its contemporaries. Perhaps also it will mean that acknowledgement of, and communion with, the Pilgrim Who Is are destined to take place in the catacombs as Bonhoeffer suggested in his occasional soundings on the meaning of the arcane discipline. With a generation that does understand our secular action and future orientation we have business to do in the modern marketplaces. But that is not all we have to do and say. The offensive code language of faith will be remembered and the Reality to which it points will be celebrated in the hidden discipline of the faith community.

Maturity

Secularization includes man's growing ability to manage his own affairs. Cox affirms this process. Reading the drive towards maturity in the light of Anabaptist, political, existential, and pragmatic components, he sees Christian faith challenged to encourage men to act in the *polis* for its humanization, and the validity of its theses tested by their effectiveness in evoking this commitment. Specifically the doctrine of God worthy of support must have these credentials:

> The doctrine of God would become theology's answer to the seemingly irrefutable fact that history can only be kept open by 'anchoring' that openness somewhere outside history itself, in this case not 'above' but *ahead*. Faith in God would be recognized for our time, in that hope for the future Kingdom of Peace that frees men to suffer and sacrifice meaningfully in the present.[22]

In this encouragement of the race's maturation towards

the Kingdom of Peace, oddly enough there may be a very subtle new invitation to immaturity. If man needs an anchor 'outside history', and such is provided by Christian eschatology, then have we not stepped back on the path of a God of the gaps? A futurized doctrine of God represents *deus ex machina* thinking to the degree that it is held out as the way men can 'make it', in this case making it in their pilgrimage towards the future.

There are at least three weaknesses in this contention.

(1) Increasingly men are demonstrating that they can find their own solutions to human quandaries, including final questions about the control of life and death which men in other ages never dared dream possible or relegated to the realm of 'religion'. It is, therefore, not unthinkable that attitude and strategies that do in fact 'keep the future open' without it being anchored outside itself in God could be evolved by man.

(2) If Christian faith encourages the coming of age of man, as we most firmly believe, then it cannot offer itself to men as a formula that is capable of doing something which man cannot by his own lights achieve. What it can do is to share whatever insights it may have on a human problem within the framework of pioneering and relinquishing. In this context, it would mean exploring eschatological themes and actions that illumine man's struggle towards the future, but encouraging at the same time secular equivalents to these insights, and displaying a readiness to recede when there is no longer any need for the gadfly and catalyst gifts the Church has to bring to the venture. We need a more radical commitment to secularization than is found in a position that holds out to man one last crutch, claiming that his future needs to be held open by the belief in One who comes, which belief saves from selfrighteousness, cynicism, utopianism, closure, etc.

(3) What makes possible a more thorough commitment to the processes of human maturation is a conviction about the nature of God that is foreclosed by an excessive wedding of theology to pragmatism. It is the belief that God is to be loved for his own sake, and that truth about him rests on grounds that are inclusive of, but not exhausted by, their problem-solving productivity. Thus in the final analysis, we speak about God who was, and is, and is to be, not because of its functionality, but because that is the way the Story goes. As that Tale is about the God who is for man, it cannot help being functional – and formulations that impede the human venture are disreputable – but in and through its serviceability it illumines the reality of One who calls us to accountability, shames us into confession, evokes a brimming thanksgiving and a resolute action. Faith is about friendship with God. Hope looks forward to him, not only because of what he can do for us, but simply because he is who he is, and will be who he will be.

Esoteric stuff for a secular age? Maybe. But, ironically, it frees us for a secular future-building and unequivocal celebration of man's coming of age. However, lest that be understood as one last desperate fling at the kind of gamesmanship we are here rejecting, let it be said that its fundamental value is that it frees us to know God as God, as One who is sought out not only for what he can do, to fill our crevices, but for who he is, a Thou to be loved in his own right.

Harvey Cox is one of the most seminal thinkers in the Church today. He has alerted Anglo-Saxon Christians to the secular city in which they must live and witness. And now he urges us towards a futurological step. We best honour his work, and that of Teilhard and Moltmann, when we press beyond provisional explorations into the larger future to which they all point.

4. Discerning the Sign of Hope

'THIS hope-talk is all well and good. But it does not add up to anything more than windy theologizing if it ends there. Just where is the hope today? Are there any signs of it that can bolster our morale? Where can we dig in with some expectation that our work for a better world will be worth the effort?'

So the empirical mind of the Anglo-Saxon world asks as it struggles through some of the intricacies of eschatology. What adds special urgency to this plea for concreteness is the state of affairs in the United States and Britain today. In the latter half of this decade many sensitive Americans have experienced a crushing despair as urban problems go begging for attention while the cities verge on explosion, white and black arm against each other, a horrible war in South-East Asia drags on, a spate of the country's most promising leaders are cut down by a violence-prone society. Meanwhile Great Britain experiences the pain of a setting sun, mounting internal discontent, and the opening wounds of bigotry. Where will it all end? Just where is this hope?

A responsible answer to this question cannot gloss over the manifest ugliness and unpromising developments either side of the Atlantic. Certainly not a Christian eschatology which has no illusions about the horrendous possibility for evil in the world. Specifically, the Christian hoper cannot assure Americans or Englishmen that 'it will turn out all right in the end' like a grade-C Hollywood romance. It is very possible that both societies will deteriorate, or destroy themselves, and possibly the rest of the world along with them by some nuclear miscalculation. Such is the freedom God has given us. And neither is Christian hope the easy counsel that 'things are not so bad after all'. To believe in hope, including its very earthly underside, does not mean that any particular slice of time and space must show clear evidence of it, particularly not in terms which are commensurate with our specific expectations. There is nothing in a Christian perspective on hope that guarantees that this moment in time in America or Britain reflects the *shalom* towards which history moves. It could be a shattered mirror fit only for the junk pile. Woe betide the false prophets who cry 'hope, hope' where there is no hope!

But paradoxically, the very despair that grips a continent and island may be a sign of promise. Suffering is a sign of hope in the biblical frame of reference: the coming of the Antichrist is a portent of the approaching fulfilment. We have included the note of sobriety as the first stage along the pilgrimage of hope wherever it is an authentic one. Thus it was necessary for the Treblinka revolutionaries to have all their false hopes wrested from them before a genuine hope could be born. Crucifixion must precede resurrection. In our present context we may say that only when the full horror of human (and cosmic) life is confronted squarely can there be any chance of healing. To the degree that the 'despair' so prevalent in both societies is an honest appraisal of how desperate things in fact are, a realism that elbows out the naïvetés to which we are regularly prone in the modern world, then we are dealing with a genuine sign of hope. Radical diagnosis is the condition for radical healing. The brutal honesty of self-criticism is evidence of a health already at work.

But *shalom* peeps through not only in the awareness that there is no *shalom*. We have argued that hope is not only in the End but in the here and there of our tattered world. The question is, can we make such claims about this particular time and place in which we now live?

The conviction expressed in this chapter is that we can. *Shalom* has left its trail even in this desert.

It is always risky to speak about such things. Does the Bible not warn us of those who say 'Lo here, lo there'? Of course, the signs of Christ's promise and presence cannot be neatly identified and classified. Not only is this true in the particularly shadowy setting in which we must today do our searching. But always, the signs are ambiguous, interlaced as they are by the frailties and forbiddingness of a world in which the powers of evil still do their work. The record of sign-seers is yet another cause for caution. They seem to be regularly proved wrong by the passage of events. Some happenings to which a set of soothsayers so confidently linked the Kingdom turn out later to be quite demonic. But in short order, another cadre of prophets arise to hail their own heroes and heroics.

It is easy to sit on the sidelines and smile at the foibles of men, and to point out the fallibilities of hopers. But the sidelines are not the angle of Christian vision. With all the risk that the quest for the divine signature in history entails, we cannot choose not to try. Christian hope, like

Christian faith, is venture and risk. On our readiness to launch out, the future depends. In fear and trembling therefore we edge towards our mandate to 'discern the signs of the times'.

The Detecting Device of Hope

We must have an instrument to locate the veins of promise on the contemporary landscape. Does the Church have such a 'Geiger counter' that can pick up the signals of the rich uranic ore of hope?

To recognize the signs of the Kingdom in our world, we must have some inkling of what they look like. And we do. What is to come has 'made the scene' in Jesus. This breakthrough is the measure of all other breakthroughs of the future. It is our device of detection and discernment.

He is our peace. In him was *Shalom*. Therefore, wherever faith finds the things that make for peace – personal, historical, natural, cosmic – there also it discovers signs of the Kingdom. We underscore *the things that make for peace*. How easy it is to pervert biblical *shalom* into sentimentality if we miss this preamble. How many false prophets have pointed to the bucolic and serene and said here is your 'peace'. But there is no peace in quiescence as such, for it may gag the cry of outraged justice. *Shalom* may be found in the righteous indignation that lashes the moneychanger, the scream of an exorcized demon, and the pain of crucifixion. The things that make for peace are those movements of Christ then and now that prepare the way for healing and embody it – the lancing of the boil, as well as the knitting together of the flesh. And without the former the latter is suspect.

The coming of *shalom* in Christ was a hard-fought struggle against the powers. We have sought to understand it as the wresting of the future from them by the second

Adam. If he is the first of a new race, then there are others to follow. The disciple will be marked by his willingness to walk through the door that Jesus widened. Following Jesus is seizing the future he opened. Wherever men are no longer cowed by the powers of closure, wherever they take their destiny in their own hands in order to make for the things of peace, there appears the seeds of the Kingdom. We look, therefore, for the readiness and power of men to accept the responsibility of their destiny, to refuse the crutch and resist the club of tyrannies, benevolent or malevolent.

Authentic self-direction in the Christian vision is not goal-less. In the abstract it can be as demonic as a peace without its preamble. It is freedom for something, freedom for man and towards *shalom*. Freedom is wed to peace in Jesus. Where men surface to claim their future in order that swords can be beaten into ploughshares, and the wolf and lamb lie down together, is found the trailmarkers towards the Kingdom.

With these hints from the centre of the Christian Story, we move to our detecting and mining. Of course, we shall not find the ore in its purity. On the kind of terrain we work, the most we can expect is low-grade mineral, alloyed by the powers of evil. In fact we may be tempted to throw away the samples we turn up. But the genuine explorer must not be turned away by the faintness of the counter's sounds. The dial shows there is something there, and we must dig.

The Freedom Revolution

The word 'freedom revolution' found its way into the modern vocabulary in the '60s to describe the surge forward of black Americans to claim their human rights.[1] Taking off from this springboard, we enlarge the rubric to include all those current struggles which bear the same marks. Wherever human beings, submerged by structures that rob them of their identity and bar the way to reconciliation, rise to take charge of their own lives and witness to the unity of mankind, a freedom revolution goes on. We have spoken of its embodiment in the life and work of Martin Luther King. Its manifestations can be seen wherever the poor surface to demand 'a say' in their destiny, where nations of rising expectation throw off the yoke of colonialism, where women refuse to accept the confinements of a male-dominated society, where the aged assert the right to be human, where workers refuse to be treated as objects of manipulation. where consumers cease to be the pawns of commercial and advertising oligarchies, where the laity move from docility under clerical domination to partnership. We select one pilgrimage towards new identity which commands increasing attention in order to discern its sign and to note as well the perils that attend every new shot of promise. Let us turn to the 'student revolution'.

Michael Novak, writing from within the campus ferment, cites one of the key factors in the revolution by quoting from a student's term paper:

> We are beginning to take seriously all those words that we have heard in sermons and commencement addresses all our lives: love, justice, liberty, equality. But those who spoke these words seem to be frightened when we take them seriously.[2]

The visions of old men follow them in their children. To speak of *shalom* is a dangerous thing, for it has a way of taking hold of receptive minds and doing its revolutionary work. The massive (though by no means universal) discontent of a younger generation with the self-seeking hypocrisy of those who preach of a world of shattered swords but continue to hurl their bombs, who orate about freedom but countenance slavery, who mouth glittering generalities about justice but cannot lift a finger to raise the oppressed, is our dream coming home to roost. No matter how we may squirm in front of our television sets and deliver little homilies on the wisdom of age, the dangers of excess, etc., the fact of the matter is that the children who march and sing are, in their most authentic moments, doing what we told them was right to do. We cannot fault them for practising the *shalom* we preached.

Of course, faith can give no uncritical blessing to any human phenomenon. The vision is still ahead, the ore is alloyed by all the frailities of men. But can the Christians among us afford not to acknowledge the fragments of the vision they are called to steward? To turn away one's own will be fatal to both father and son.

The student revolution in its most creative expression is more than witness to *shalom*. It is the movement upward of a smothered humanity towards that goal. When young adults – who are that, well before an older generation credits them as such – decide they will not be treated as children, then all our solemn theological talk about coming of age is seen for what it really means. If a young man can be given a gun by a Government that considers him mature enough to know when to shoot it at other people, he is mature enough to have a say in the life of his academic community. Autocracy in any form is intolerable in a world come of age, including the benign paternalism that has so long gone unchallenged in educational establishments. Where a student generation reaches for partnership in the academic venture, its struggle will be welcomed by those who believe in the right of the VLP to challenge the VIP, whether the VLP be the poor, the black, the female, the new nation, the consumer, the old, or the young. And the believer will seek, as well, in the struggle for co-determination, a sign of the Kingdom.

We speak of co-determination and partnership. The tragic side of a freedom revolution, the peril that plagues the promise, is the lust for hegemony. It makes its appearance in the resistance of the tyrant to the new surge forward. But it is found as well in the revolutionary when he seeks to topple the tyranny only to establish a new one. Often out of frustration with the implacability of the Establishment, as much as out of the corruptions of new power, the legitimate cry for black presence and power turns to black messianism, the demand for worker participation explodes into a shout for worker dictatorship, and the affirmation of student power and participatory democracy sours into demands for student control. This is a betrayal of authentic revolution because it divorces freedom from *shalom*. In the Christian vision, the goal towards which freedom bends its efforts is the healing of the rifts which rupture creation. To use the power of self-determination to grind another's face into the ground is fresh captivity to the powers of evil. Those who resist the struggle of the voiceless to find their voice, and thus plant the seeds of a despair that propels towards the new monologue, are just as culpable as those who succumb to it. How desperately we need in this revolution, as in the others, the presence and testimony of the Christian vision which marries freedom to reconciliation.

There is another point at which the Christian testimony can serve the student revolution: the de-ideologizing of the struggle. Many of the more colourful European 'megaphones'[3] of student protest interpret and encourage the movement in orthodox Marxist categories (although not conventional Communist terms). The Continental tradition of assimilating historical ferment into neat systems, and its affinity for abstractions, persists even in a youthful revolution anxious to shatter all connexions with the past. Faith cannot place its final confidence in human constructs that claim to explain and map out the future with the details that are so readily available to the ideologue. The historical future belongs to that unpredictable creature, Man, who may find solutions to his problems that confound the cleverest of dogmas. Or he may blow it up. Also, fixing its ultimate commitment to that One who is outside and ahead of the penultimate arena, faith can never give itself over uncritically to any finite passion, Marxist or otherwise.

The practical effect of this de-ideologizing is that it frees the participant in the student revolution to see it as a struggle against tyranny, the course of which must be worked out as it proceeds in terms of the specific issues that arise. It throws off the shackles of a theory that has already schematized tomorrow. The future is open.

As we have discovered before in the household conversation on hope, whatever the Christian community has to offer in a secular dialogue is in the context of the pioneering and provisional. The task of de-ideologizing can, in principle, be done by human insight, and should finally be done just that way in a world come of age. Thus, an empirical 'let's see as we go along' modesty, which increasingly characterizes the approach of a technological society to its problems, has its witness to bear to the solution of social problems. We work through answers to the questions that press upon us without attempting to fit them into grandiose formulations. This may be the direction in which the Christian vision can be responsibly secularized.

A further perspective that Christian hope brings to the student revolution has to do with the question of violence. There is no place in the End for man to lift up his hand against his neighbour. *Shalom*, by definition, is without violence. The conscience of faith is always guided by this vision, and stung by it when it is violated.

Of course, hope knows that the perfect dream of End-time *shalom* cannot be transported in packaged fashion into history. In the kingdom of Heaven love is triumphant, self-giving evokes self-giving, and reconciliation is the issue, However, on the plane of the penultimate, where the powers of evil have not been cast out, self-giving does not always evoke self-giving, but in fact may invite exploitation of the giver or the defenceless who rely upon him. Perfect love in this world goes to the cross. Therefore the defence of the weak, with the tragic violence that it may entail, cannot be ruled out *a priori*. With the depths of a Treblinka we have reached that point.

Because hope recognizes violence as one of the signs of a fallen world, it can never rest easy with this recourse, nor build it into its strategies for social change, nor countenance aggressive violence. The Kingdom draws us towards those methods consonant with its life. And they may be militant ones including demonstration, march, boycott, sit-in, and a civil disobedience as prepared to take the consequences for its action as St. Paul. But these are not the way of the clenched fist, the club or the gun.

The disavowal of violence as a strategy for social change is a Christian instinct whose secular vindication becomes increasingly clear. Violence in a technological society is more and more shown up to be counter-productive of genuine revolution in freedom. A violence-prone country such as the United States comes into disrepute before the world community for the horror of its actions overseas and in the shame of its gun-hoarding and sniper-ridden domestic life. Moreover, violence, when adopted by desperate minorities driving towards social change, only serves to produce the reaction of a more powerfully armed and vicious majority. Most perilous of all is the fact that in an advanced technological society techniques of killing and maiming – from chemicals to miniaturized A-bombs – have been so perfected, and have become so accessible to those who want to use them and so vulnerable to accidental possibilities, that the countenancing of violence in a programme for social change courts disaster for both the revolution and the society as a whole. The Christian and the thoughtful freedom fighter must join hands to carry out the work of peaceful revolution.

'Freedom is a constant struggle' says the freedom song of a freedom revolution. Twice so, for the cadres of Christian hopers. It is a struggle to discern the authentic movements of liberation. And it is a difficult job to march in their ranks, not in rigid conformity to their music but to 'the beat of a distant drummer'. But the pilgrim whose eyes are forward must take the risk and do it.

The Fashioning of Life

The Socratic counsel, 'Know thyself', is obsolete, says José Delgado. The Yale brain researcher who has made history with experiments in electrode manipulation of animal behaviour lifts up a new fighting word: Fashion thyself.[5]

Our theological abstractions about 'coming of age' gain fresh pungency as reports filter out of the laboratories about man's new power to reshape his nature and destiny. While the sceptic grunts, 'Science fiction', and the conservative scoffs at 'blue sky' forecasts, pioneering exploration goes on apace.

Landmark innovation in which man reaches to do things formerly assigned to providence or fate falls into three categories as they touch upon human existence: (1) *the creation of life*, ranging from uniting sperm and ovum outside the human womb and cultivating its growth there, through tissue culture looking towards the replication of body parts, to the decoding and rewriting of the DNA story; (2) *the extension of life* running from indefinite preservation by 'freezing' through the slowing down of the ageing process, the extensive use of transplant and synthetic organs, to the grisly prospect of continued existence as an 'isolated perfuse head'; and (3) *the direction of life*, including the arrangement of shape, colour, size, skills, intelligence, personality, peace of mind and 'love of God' by prenatal surgery, electrode implantation, radiation or computer brain control, and drugs.

What are we to make of these awesome possibilities? Harassed by the powers of evil, subject to the perils of any new power, they are, nevertheless, signs of a vast new hope. By the test of our two-pronged diving rod, they emerge as eschatological portents.

Life-changing developments in science-technology are bold steps forward in man's pilgrimage to maturity. To the extent that man presses forward to manage his own future he 'grows up into Christ'. As Christ contested the powers and removed their grip on the future, he beckons men to follow where he led captivity captive. Human action that accepts no limits to its vista, and therefore seeks to 'construct itself', is living out the call of Christ to pass through the door he opened. As the Kingdom erupted in his action, its lava flows wherever men seek to fashion their future.

The freedom and work of Christ were bent towards the service of *shalom*. The Kingdom comes when men are made whole and the creation no longer groans. Where the new powers are harnessed for healing, there are fertilizing the seeds of a New Creation. To mend life, to add to both its quantity and quality, to raise it to undreamed-of levels – we inch towards these ends and sometimes stride towards them by means of our science-technology. Can we say that these goals have nothing to do with The Goal? Not by New

Testament reckoning. They are sacraments of the End in which its Lord and his gifts are present. We celebrate their coming!

But it is a sober celebration. The capacity to fashion life is no more an unmixed blessing than the freedom revolution. The signs are disfigured by the evil powers that still have enough life to carve their initials on the creative works of men. Therefore, the faith community joins the exhilarating press forward, but not uncritically. It plays out its uncomfortable gadfly role. It asks embarrassing questions. For example: What does an electrode implantation, a drug or a yet-unpredictable form of bio-control do to the field of freedom? Perhaps it would reason: If the innovation eliminates a factor that has impaired the exercise of choice (an electrode that allays a debilitating pain or epileptic pattern), making possible a new serenity, let there be rejoicing. Such exorcism of a demonic power is Christ's own healing ministry in modern dress. On the other hand, a device that would prestructure the choosing life of a person, thus programming 'virtue', would raise serious questions about the consequences for the human factor.

In the uprush of innovation the faith community makes its witness to freedom with regard to matters of society as well as self. Will those affected by the technological revolution have a say in its social uses, especially those at whom 'improvements' might be directly aimed? The ugly implementation of new technology in the Hitler era is an example of what can happen when decision-making is vested in *élite* groups.

The same thing could happen, however, in democratic societies by subtler and/or more haphazard events. Middle class scientists meeting in their professional societies to address themselves conscientiously to the ethical use of a new discovery, or clergy, scientists, politicians and industrialists gathering with the best of intentions in 'evangelical academies' to work out middle axioms for innovations may be courting a dehumanization no less fearful than the Nazi horror.

What is missing in these well-intentioned conclaves of the VIPs is the presence and voice of the VLPs. When the question of eliminating juvenile delinquency in a slum area by bio-control appears on the agenda, shall we leave the decision to the wise and the mighty? A faith that affirms man's right to control his own destiny in a world whose future has been opened by Christ – and that also has no illusions about the objectivity of the bright, the pious, and the powerful – will stand up to be counted for the voice of the voiceless in the councils of decision.

There is another orange traffic signal amid the green along the way to the future of life-controlling developments. It has also to do with Christian testimony about the human factor. This time we mean in its street sense: 'After all he's only human'. In the code language of faith, man is a sinner.

A Niebuhrian realism ought to be a welcome companion to those who live in the uprush of scientific advance. A sober realization of the catastrophic as well as the ennobling possibilities in man's use of his new power will point to the building of safeguards into the innovative and operating processes, safeguards such as the democratizing of decision-making suggested earlier.

In addition to the pragmatic value of an astringent realism, there is the effect it has on our attitude to the future. In affirming the contribution of science-technology we have spoken of whetted expectations, But this is a sober hope that does not rest its final confidence in a utopia brought off tomorrow by an ethically sure-footed toolmaker. As we have noted before, growing up does not mean moral maturity in the human community any more than it does in the individual who becomes 21. Reaching towards the adulthood of the race through the capacity to manage the future by human action could be as disastrous as the arrival for the first time at voting age in order to cast a ballot for the hate-mongering candidate.

In yet another sense, the faith community brings its 'man-talk' into the life-fashioning currents. There are scientists who say, 'My job is being a good scientist. Somebody else will have to worry about the uses to which my work is put.' The scientist has set loose vast forces that affect the destiny of man, including his own progeny. He lives on no island, and can crawl into no cave of specialism that insulates itself from the human impact of his discoveries.

Helmut Thielicke has shown the devastating effects of the 'technician mentality' of the professional in the Hitler era who acceded to the totalitarian state by abdicating the asking of the 'why' and 'to what end' questions. He became a 'fountain pen, technically a highly qualified writing instrument, but empty, and writes equally well with brown, red, or black ink, depending upon what is pumped into it.'6 Alert scientists are of course aware of the dangers of this moral monasticism, as witness the *Bulletin of the Atomic Scientists*. In any case, one of the notes that the Church must strike in its partnership with the accelerating capacity of man to fashion himself is the reminder to every occupation of its responsibility for the effects of its work on the human future.

As in the freedom revolution, so here in what we might call the 'life revolution' the Church struggles to be faithful to its difficult double role. It celebrates the signs of hope and ranges itself alongside those who embody them. But it never lets its critical faculty wilt in the heat of involvement. Its eyes cannot come to rest on anything less than the

131

End, and it gives its heart alone to the God out ahead of the most expansive plans and dreams of men.

The Turning of the Church

Something happened to the Church in the '60s. A pope opened a window and called a council. Clergy and laity were at the head of picket lines and behind jail bars. Martyrdom found its way once again into the language of faith. Christian presence made itself felt on the factory floor, in the council chamber, the streets, the high rise apartments, the coffee houses, among statesman and revolutionaries. An old word shone with new lustre: 'God so loved the world . . .'; 'Go into all the world . . .'; 'You are the light of the world . . .' Many within the Church did an about-face *metanoia* and marched in a new direction. This movement towards the *world* to bear witness to *shalom*, was also a movement towards the End, and therefore an eschatological sign.

Re-orientation meant turning away from something, an era of incurvature. Post war Christendom had its prophets, but its heart belonged to the priests of the inner sanctum, They presided over the cult of peace of mind which transmuted Christian faith into a message of inner tranquillity which uncritically accepted or blessed the *status quo* of a dog-eat-dog society, They worshipped at the shrine of the Goddess of Getting-ahead. The big membership, the busy programme, the imposing new building and the hefty budget became the test of faithfulness, not to the God who had no place to lay his head, but to the bitch goddess of success. There was the cult of sophisticated existential quandary which spent itself in spiritual navel-gazing, mesmerized by the internal puzzles of meaninglessness, anxiety and despair. There was the cult of pietism whose bombast offered personal rescue from fire and brimstone but knew nothing of the full Gospel's promise of a reconciled *world*, and the challenge to prepare for it here and now. There was the cult of 'groupiness' which thrived in the self-serving coteries of culture-Protestantism or in ecclesiastical ideologies which viewed the Church rather than the Kingdom as the goal of mission. Penitents turned their back on these 'I, me, mine' preoccupations, calling for a 'Church for others', a movement from an inward-looking Christendom to an outward-looking servanthood.

Lending urgency to neighbour-oriented style were the stakes of human ministration which modern technology had pushed upward fantastically. With his powerful new instruments of construction or destruction, and living in a tightly woven web of interdependence, modern man could ennoble or devastate his home according to the path chosen. Wars are fought not with bows and arrows but in megatons and with population-destroying chemicals. Poverty becomes intolerable in a world of plenty. Medical advances drip with promise which must be made available to all. In a global village with a Jericho road running through it, the first business of the Church is to do what the Lord commands in such circumstances – 'bind up wounds'. The neighbour-love ministry cries out to be the arrow-head of mission.

Worldly mission is influenced by yet another contemporary factor, the growing understanding of how wounds are, in fact, bound up in a complex 20th century setting. Meaningful service had to go to the roots of vast problems and not be content with palliatives. The 'plantation charity' of the new North as well as the old South obscures and aggravates wounds that can only be healed by the elimination of the welfare system as well as the slave system. A Church keyed to mission in the world knows that social structures impede or facilitate the coming of *shalom*, and therefore is

133

prepared to challenge the 'principalities and powers' and work for their conversion. It is here that some of the hottest sparks fly as new Nathans confront the Davids of the day with the charge, 'Thou art the man', and the fiery furnaces continue to be stoked by modern Nebuchadnezzars.

The shape taken by this thrust into the world is often that of a 'new form' of mission and ministry. Thus the industrial mission, the movement or *ad hoc* group struggling for human rights, the urban missioner, the poverty worker, the renewal centre, the coffee house, the urban training centre, the leisure ministry, the town and country institute, the campus chaplain, the task force within a congregation or denomination, the new congregation built around focus on a human need, the centre for 'abandonment ministries' within a cooperative parish are a few of the variety of ways in which world-oriented mission finds its way into the life of the Church.

And why would the appearance of these new forms and the things they represent be a sign of promise? What does reforming an educational system, or the push for civil rights legislation, or the struggle to secure the voice of the poor in their own destiny have to do with a more hopeful Church? For one, where men rise to take responsibility for their future and mould it to the design of a reconciled world, they set up signs to the End. But there is another quality in this act that makes the contemporary witness of the Christian community a sign of hope, over and above its kinship with the secular foretastes dealt with previously. When the church is 'involved', its action is within the framework of its confession of Jesus and his Kingdom. Church action, therefore, is the conscious living testimony to its message, an enactment of its Story. And as faithful proclamation, it walks the way of the Herald who *was* his message, an incarnate Word. As it stumbles out on the

Jericho thoroughfares to bind up wounds, a turned Church is a parable of the action of the One who comes. When deed marries Word, we celebrate a sign of hope.*

Polarization

In the race towards the world some move faster than others. The distance between the front runners and those who bring up the rear takes its toll. It appears in the Church today as a polarization between those committed to turning, and those who want to do business as usual. In fact, some forecast a new split within the Christian community along these lines, replacing denominational division and over-shadowing conventional ecumenical interests (although bringing to birth a new ecumenism around a common addressment to the human issues). Already there is a tend-ency for this division to crystallize in terms of those active in new forms and those who work in more traditional church structures. It is manifest as well in the emergence of group-ings of 'committed', either outside established ecclesiastical forms, as new congregations 'stripped down to fighting weight', as cells within conventional church life, or as some variety of 'underground church'.

It is not the first time in the history of Christian com-munal life that this kind of internal tension has taken place. Lessons from this experience may be able to help us make

* The Church as an eschatological community is a favourite theme in the growing literature on Christian hope. Perfectionist groups and those stressing radical mission or stringent membership standards lay particular claim to the label on the grounds that they seek to embody without qualification the vision of an untainted life for others. There is historical precedent for this assertion, as witness the close links between eschatology and ethics in separatist movements. In the Catholic tradition also there is some basis for interpreting the order, with its vows of poverty, celibacy and radical obedience, as uncompromisingly antici-patory of the End, and therefore eschatological. We have taken a different tack here declining to narrow the eschatological circle to elite groups alone. As the theme is developed in these pages, the ordinary as well as the extraordinary can participate through an electing love in eschatological processes.

creative use of it. And learning from contemporary secular institutional life may also be able to contribute. Otherwise polarization can seriously impair the fruitfulness of the signs of renewal in the Church.

When a religious Establishment resists its prophetic minorities, it does so at its own peril; for it empties its ranks of its most creative spirits, and denies itself the self-criticism that it needs to adapt to changing circumstances. This is eminently so in a period of accelerated change, as students of social institutions in a technological society regularly point out in their recommendation of 'self-imposed disrupters' and 'critics-in-residence'.[7] But here our main concern is with the corruptions of a sign of promise, and hence with the risks within secular mission. Thus, when the creative minority, frustrated by the inaction or attacks of the Establishment, decides to opt out, it does a profound disservice to its own cause. What is involved is more than the pragmatic consideration that vast church resources which might be harnessed for mission are being bypassed, although this is indeed a factor. The history of sect movements is a tale of withdrawals that not only impoverish the main stem of the Church but also thin the identity of the separatist, and thus weaken his witness. Gathered into its own enclave, its message and style invariably are pared to fit its particular sensitivities and circumstances, and the fullness of its Christian testimony shrivels to these proportions. Identity is further attenuated often (although not always, as the sect may remain aloof from cultural contact) by the ease with which a reduced Christianity makes itself at home on missionary terrain, having disengaged itself from the historical identity symbols of the larger Christian community which transcends that environment. Communication slips into accommodation. Alongside the ideological dangers, there is the temptation to which elitism is particularly vulnerable, the pharisaical breast-beating which disdains the Christian masses: 'thank God, I am not as other men!'

There is an option in ecclesiology other than those of the uncritical Establishment and the separatist enclave. It is a partnership in mission. The conventional church constituency must discover that it needs its critics-in-residence, its scouts on worldly terrain, its research centres, in order to keep itself alive to its missionary Gospel, and to be assured of catalysis of mission. It should spin loose, work in conjunction with, and keep itself open to the new directions charted by the map-makers, the new forms and task forces geared to pioneering the human tasks. And the cadres of secular missionaries must keep in range of, and in living relationship to, its institutional brethren. After a period of mutual excommunication, there is some significant evidence that this kind of alliance is, in fact, developing. Thus the ordinary and the extraordinary, the weak and the strong, the fast and the slow, the wheat and the tares, grow together in the kind of creative tension appropriate to the Christian organism.[8]

To Mute or Not to Mute the Message

A second risk that attends the turning Church is the weakening of its kerygmatic ministry. A variety of factors play their parts here. The sheer weight of meeting basic human needs is so demanding that less and less time is devoted to the verbalization and celebration of faith. On the Jericho road, the Samaritan did not preach any sermons. Again, in a secular society, the language of transcendence is either met with blank stares, or heard mistakenly through the sounds of outmoded association. Further in an age shaped by 'cool' media the acts of visible involvement cut more ice than the print-idea complex in which the *kerygma* has been conventionally cast. And finally, the deeper the penetration of secular land, and the more separatist the disengagement from the centres of Christian language, the less comfortable the worldly missionary becomes with his inherited symbols. It is not surprising, therefore, that the call is sounded for a moratorium on God-talk, or for its abandonment, and for mission re-interpreted exclusively in terms of the secular acts of compassion and justice.

There are many situations in which the act of mission is the simple act of human care. Social action has an integrity of its own. Further, in a secular society with sky-high human stakes, the tip point of mission is a Church turned to others. But mission as a total strategy of the Christian community is not exhausted by social action. Put in its simplest terms, the love of God is inseparable from the love of neighbour, but one is not reducible to the other. Within the love of God comes confession and thanksgiving to him, the telling of his Story and the celebration of his action. There is a life with God that goes on in, with, and under the life with the neighbour.

This life with God will find its main expression in a secular society by way of hidden discipline that takes place in the closets of personal devotion and the catacombs of the faith community. It will also spill over on the secular landscape wherever the symbols of faith can illumine the human issues. And it will tumble out too, even when unsolicited by our contemporaries and offensive to them.

Our exercise in eschatology has been just this kind of Story-telling. The ancient tale is first and foremost for the ears of faith, for those drawn to these symbols in quest of their 20th-century identity and mission. Embarrassing talk about the End will cut little ice with those who have eyes and ears alone for empirical immediacies. However, as we have sought to show, there is a growing alliance of the End-oriented even within the secular community itself, and they will not find the noises we make altogether strange. It is even possible that Christian futurity and modern futurisms that refuse to be captive to the *status quo* can be something of a 'lobby for the future', and that such a partnership may constitute itself a sign of hope.

As we began this book with a poem expressing an eschatological demurrer, we conclude with one that sees a little way farther up ahead. Taking off from a freedom revolution, it speaks the language of a new eschatology that puts its question mark over what is, in the light of a vision of things to come, and the One who holds it before our eyes;

> One of these days
> Somebody is going to ask, 'Why?'
> 'Why' is a bad word,
> A dirty word.
> It must never be uttered, or even thought.
> Especially not thought.
> Four letter words are not the worst words;
> The really bad words are three letter words.
> Powerful words like 'sex'.
> Terrible words like 'God'.
> And 'why' is a truly dreadful word.
> '*Why* is there meat and fruit
> And liquor and ice for you?'
> '*Why* is there nothing but greasy grits
> And flour and beans for me?'
> When someone starts asking why
> It is already too late to hide.
> *Why* is the switch that lights up the end of the world.[9]

Selected Bibliography

CURRENT CONVERSATION ON CHRISTIAN FUTURITY

Robert Adolfs *The Grave of God: Has the Church a Future?* translated by N. D. Smith, Burns & Oates, London 1967: especially chapters 2, 5

Gregory Baum (ed.) *The Future of Belief Debate* Herder & Herder, New York 1967

*Ernst Benz *Evolution and Christian Hope: Man's Concept of the Future from the Early Fathers to Teilhard de Chardin* translated by Heinz G. Frank, Doubleday & Co., Garden City, N.Y. 1966; Gollancz, London 1967

Peter Berger *A Rumor of Angels* Doubleday & Co., Garden City, N.Y. 1966, especially chapter 5

Hendrikus Berkhof *Christ, the Meaning of History* translated by Lambertus Burrman, S.C.M. Press, London 1966

Blanchette, Cox, Dewart *et al.*, *Christian Initiative in History* The Church Society for College Work 1967

*Ernst Bloch *Das Prinzip der Hoffnung* vols 1, 2, Frankfurt; Suhokamp Verlag 1959

Carl Braaten *History and Hermeneutics* Lutterworth Press, London 1968

Rudolf Bultmann *History and Eschatology* The Gifford Lectures 1955, University Press, Edinburgh 1957; Harper Torchbooks, New York 1957

Rudolf Bultmann and Karl Rentdorf *Hope* Adams and Charles Bles, London 1963

*Walter Capps (ed.) symposium 'Hope' *Cross Currents* Summer 1968 Vol. LXVIII No. 3

Kenneth Cauthen *Science, Secularization and God* Abingdon Press, Nashville 1969

*Harvey Cox *On Not Leaving it to the Snake* Macmillan Co., New York 1967; S.C.M. Press, London 1968

Harvey Cox, Helmut Gollwitzer, Kenneth Heinitz, Jürgen Moltmann 'The Christian-Marxist Dialogue' *Dialog* Vol. 7 Winter 1968

Oscar Cullmann *Salvation in History* translated by Sidney Sowers and afterward completed by the editorial staff of the S.C.M., Harper & Row, New York 1967; S.C.M. Press, London 1967

Charles Davis *A Question of Conscience* Hodder & Stoughton, London 1967: especially pp. 99–117, 181–241

*Leslie Dewart *The Future of Belief* Burns & Oates, London 1966

Christianity and Crisis 28 no. 14 (5 August 1968): 'Christian Realism: a Symposium'

Gabriel Fackre *Secular Impact: The Promise of Mission* United Church Press, Philadelphia, Pa. 1968: especially chapters 10, 11

*Roger Garaudy *From Anathema to Dialogue* with replies by Karl Rahner s.j. and J. B. Metz, Collins, London 1967

Gerhard Gloege *The Day of His Coming* translated by Stanley Rudman, Fortress Press, Philadelphia, Pa. 1963

*Cameron Hall (compiler) *Human Values and Advancing Technology* Friendship Press, New York 1967

William Hamilton and Thomas J. J. Altizer *Radical Theology and the Death of God* Bobbs-Merrill, Indianapolis, Ind. 1966: especially pp. 95–110, 121–169

Karl Heim *The World: Its Creation and Consummation* translated by Robert Smith, Oliver & Boyd, London 1962

J. C. Hoekendijk *The Church Inside Out* edited by L. A. Hoedemaker & Pieter Tijmes, translated by Isaac C. Rottenberg, Westminster Press, Philadelphia, Pa. 1966

Gerald Jud *Pilgrims Process* United Church Press, Philadelphia, Pa. 1967

*William Lynch *Images of Hope* New American Library, New York 1965

*Hans Jochen Margull *Hope in Action* translated by Eugene Peters, Muhlenberg Press, Philadelphia, Pa. 1962

Wolf-Dieter Marsch *et al.*, *Discussion über die Theologie der Hoffnung von Jürgen Moltmann* Christian Kaiser Verlag, München 1967

Gabriel Marcel *Homo Viator: Introduction to a Metaphysics of Hope* trans. Emma Graufurd, Harper Torchbooks, New York 1962

James Martin *The Last Judgment in Protestant Theology from Orthodoxy to Ritschl* Introduction by T. F. Torrance, Wm B. Eerdmans Co., Grand Rapids, Mich. 1963

*Martin Marty and Dean Peerman (eds) *New Theology* no. 5, Macmillan, New York 1968

Martin Marty *The Search for a Usable Future* Harpers, New York 1969

Sister Mary Corita *Footnotes and Headlines* Herder & Herder, New York 1968

E. L. Mascall *The Christian Universe* Darton, Longman & Todd, London 1966

Johannes Metz *Toward a Theology of the World* Herder & Herder, New York 1969

*Jürgen Moltmann *Theology of Hope* translated by James W. Leitch, S.C.M. Press, London 1967

*Christopher F. Mooney s.j. *Teilhard de Chardin and the Mystery of Christ* Collins, London 1966

S. Mowinckel *He that Cometh* translated by G. W. Anderson, Basil Blackwell, Oxford 1959

Maryellen Muckenhirn (ed. and introduction by) *The Future as the Presence of a Shared Hope* Sheed & Ward, New York 1968

142

Bernard Olivier *Christian Hope* Newman Press. Westminster, Md. 1963
★Wolfhart Pannenberg *Jesus: God and Man* translated by Lewis L. Wilkins & Duane Priebe, Westminster Press, Philadelphia, Pa. 1968
Josef Pieper *The End of Time: A Meditation on the Philosophy of History* translated by Michael Bullock, Faber & Faber, London 1954
Karl Rahner S.J. *The Christian of the Future* Burns & Oates, London 1967
—— *Theological Investigations* vol. 4, translated by Kevin Smythe, Darton, Longman & Todd, London 1966: especially pp. 323–354
—— *Theological Investigations* vol. 5, translated by Karl-H. Kruger, Darton, Longman & Todd, London 1966: especially pp. 135–192
Rosemary Reuther *The Church Against Itself* Sheed & Ward, London 1967
Dietrich Ritschl *Memory and Hope* Macmillan Co., New York 1967
James Robinson and John Cobb (eds) *Theology as History* vol. iii: *New Frontiers in Theology* Harper & Row, New York 1967
J. A. T. Robinson *In the End God* Collins: Fontana Books, London 1968
Stephen Rose *Alarms and Visions* Renewal Magazine, Chicago 1967
★Gerhard Sauter *Zukunft und Verheissung* Zwingli Verlag, Zürich 1965
★E. Schillebeeckx, O.P. *God and the Future of Man* Sheed and Ward, New York 1968
Albert Schweitzer *The Kingdom of God in Primitive Christianity* edited with an Introduction by Ulrich Neuenschwander, translated by L. A. Garrard, Adam & Charles Black, London 1968
James Sellers *Theological Ethics* Macmillan Co., New York 1966
Ronald Gregor Smith *Secular Christianity* Collins, London 1966; Harper & Row, New York 1966: especially pp. 89–131
★*The Student World* 61 no. 2 (September 1968): 'Toward the Future'
Pierre Teilhard de Chardin S.J. *The Future of Man* translated by Norman Denny, Collins, London 1964
—— *Le Milieu Divin* Collins: Fontana Books, London 1964
★—— *The Phenomenon of Man* Collins: Fontana Books, London 1965
Helmut Thielicke *Theological Ethics* vol. 1, edited by William H. Lazerth, Fortress Press, Philadelphia, Pa. 1966
W. A. Visser 't Hooft *Christians for the Future* British Broadcasting Co. 1967
★Gerhard von Rad *Old Testament Theology* vol. ii, translated by D. M. G. Stalker, Oliver & Boyd, London 1965
★Western Working Group and North American Working Group *The Church for Others and the Church for the World* World Council of Churches, Geneva 1966
Amos Wilder *Kerygma, Eschatology and Ethics* Fortress Press, Philadelphia, Pa. 1966.
George Huntston Williams *The Radical Reformation* Westminster Press, Philadelphia, Pa. 1962

★ Indicates studies of special importance.

1 'Eschatology', by Morris Bishop in *The Pocket Book of Verse* gathered, sifted, salted and with an introduction by David McCord (Pocket Books Inc., New York 1945), p. 135

2 Harvey Cox *On Not Leaving it to the Snake* p. 66

3 Vernard Eller, 'Protestant Radicalism' *The Christian Century* vol. lxxxiv, no. 44 (1 November 1967), p. 1393; see also his sequel, 'Comments on an Unsolicited Series' *The Christian Century* vol. lxxxv, no. 15 (10 April 1968), pp. 459–60, in which he argues that the new eschatological emphasis is better identified as a 'theology of promise' that accents the divine initiative rather than the more anthropocentric 'theology of hope'. We retain the 'hope' description without hesitation not only because it has good biblical credentials but because we need a more dialectical understanding of the relation of the divine and the human than is suggested by the Eller formulation.

4 quoted in Bernard Olivier *Christian Hope* page v

5 Karl Menninger. 'Hope' in *The American Journal of Psychiatry* (December 1959), pp. 481ff.; see also his book *The Vital Balance* (Viking Press, New York 1963) Cf. also William F. Lynch *Images of Hope* (London 1965)

6 For a running account of current developments in futurology, see *The Futurist: A Newsletter for Tomorrow's World*, published by the World Future Society. We shall examine this point of view in more detail in Chapter 1. PO Box 19285, Twentieth Station, Washington, D.C. 20036

7 see Charles H. Kener and Benjamin B. Tregoe *The Rational Manager: A Systematic Approach to Problem Solving and Decision Making* (McGraw-Hill, New York 1965) and William R. Ewald Jr (ed.) *Environment for Man: The Next Fifty Years* (Indiana University Press 1967) for a sampling of planning perspective; for an imaginative application of planning to massive urban problems, see the literature of the Los Angeles Goals Project: Los Angeles Planning Department, *Goals*; Los Angeles Planning Department, *Goals and Reality*; Inter-Religious Committee, Los Angeles Goals Project, *Why Not: Social and Human Goals for the Los Angeles Region*.

8 José Delgado's phrase; see his essay, 'Brain Technology and Psychocivilization', in *Human Values and Advancing Technology* pp. 68–92; see also G. Rattray Taylor *The Biological Time Bomb* (Thames & Hudson, London 1968)

9 for example, Howard and Harriet Kurtz, 'Global Compassionate Power' *Renewal* (June 1967); Michael Harrington 'A Hope', *The Accidental Century* (Butterworth)

10 as in the folk music of Pete Seeger, Sydney Carter, Josh White, Joan Baez and Paul Simon, and the art of Mary Corita Kent ('Sister Corita')

11 see the series, 'Students in Revolt' *The Times* (London) 27 May–1 June 1968

12 Roger Garaudy *From Anathema to Dialogue*; *Dialog:* The Christian–Marxist Dialogue, vol. vii, no. 1 (Winter 1968)
Roger Garaudy and Quentin Laner s.j., *A Christian–Communist Dialogue* (Garden City, Doubleday and Co. 1968); Dialogue between Christians and Marxists, *Study Encounter* IV.1.1968

13 The Second Assembly of the World Council of Churches *The Evanston Report* (SCM Press. London 1955) and *The Report of the Advisory Council of the Main*

Theme of the Second Assembly (Harper, New York 1954). Hans Jochen Margull gives a good overview of the development of eschatology in World Council circles in *Hope in Action*. For a line of thought germinated in the ecumenical movement that has since been very influential in the eschatological thinking of church renewal leaders, see J. C. Hoekendijk *The Church Inside Out*.

14 Oscar Cullmann *Christ and Time* revised edition, translated by Floyd V. Filson (SCM Press, London 1962) and his later *Salvation in History*.

15 In addition to sections in their major systematic works, see Emil Brunner *Eternal Hope* (Westminster Press, Philadelphia 1954); Karl Barth *Community, State and Church* with an introduction by Will Herberg (Doubleday & Co., Garden City, New York 1960); Paul Tillich, 'The Right to Hope' *The University of Chicago Magazine* (November 1965), pp. 16–21. See also Reinhold Niebuhr *The Nature and Destiny of Man* 2 vols (Nisbet, London 1939, 1940) *passim;* H. Richard Niebuhr *The Kingdom of God in America* (Shoestring Press, Hamden, Conn. 1956); Karl Heim *The World: its Creation and Consummation* Nicolas Berdyaev *The Beginning and the End* (Geoffrey Bles, London 1952)

16 Anonymous author quoted in Bennett Cerf, *Out of a Limerick* (Harper & Bros, New York 1960) p. 20

17 For other introductory overviews of the theology of hope, see Walter Capps, 'The Hope Tendency', in the *Cross Currents* issue on the new eschatology, and 'Introduction' and *passim* in Martin Marty and Dean Peerman, *New Theology*, No. 5, New York, the Macmillan Company, 1968.

CHAPTER I

1 Martin Luther King *Chaos or Community?* (Hodder & Stoughton, London 1968), pp. 102–3, 119–20

2 Speech to Memphis trashmen, 3 April 1968, recorded by BBC 1

3 Speech to Washington March, 28 August 1963

4 King *Chaos or Community?* p. 1

5 ibid., p. 16

6 ibid., loc. cit.

7 ibid., p. 94

8 ibid., Dedication

9 ibid., p. 124

10 ibid., p. 90

11 ibid., p. 138

12 Herman Kahn & Anthony J. Weiner *The Year* 2000: *A Framework for Speculation on the Next Thirty-Three Years* (Macmillan, New York 1967), Introduction, p. xxiv

13 see also the comments of Herbert Marcuse *One-Dimensional Man* (Beacon Press, Boston 1964; Routledge & Kegan Paul, London 1964), pp. 80–3

14 Kahn & Weiner *The Year* 2000 p. 116, quoting p. 51

15 ibid., p. 412

16 For the components, see ibid., p. 7. The authors distinguish between a 'naïve' projection rooted in the bare givens, and their own more sophisticated use of present data which tries to anticipate deviations from present trends as these are affected by the very technological innovations implicit in the present situation. The difference between the two is illustrated by the more modest population figures projected than those currently put forward on the basis of

current rates of increase, because the former takes account into account innovation in birth control that may affect significantly the present trend.

[17] ibid., p. 412

[18] ibid., Introduction, p. xxviii

[19] ibid., p. 358

[20] ibid., p. 413. Cf. 'Faust and the Future; An Interview with Anthony J. Weiner', *Tempo*, National Council of Churches, vol. 2, no. 6 (1 January 1969) pp. 6–7

[21] 'The Right to Hope', op. cit., p. 19

[22] Comment on BBC 2 interview with J. R. R. Tolkien, 30 March 1968

[23] J. R. R. Tolkien *The Fellowship of the Ring* rev. edn (Allen & Unwin, London 1966), Foreword, pp. 6–7

[24] BBC 2 interview, 30 March 1968

[25] Tolkien *The Two Towers* rev. edn (Allen & Unwin, London 1966), p. 90

[26] Tolkien *The Return of the King* rev. edn (Allen & Unwin, London 1966), p. 211

[27] Tolkien *The Road Goes Ever On* Poems set to music by Donald Swann (Allen & Unwin, London 1968)

[28] ibid.

[29] *The Return of the King* loc. cit.

[30] *The Two Towers* loc. cit.

[31] ibid., p. 31

[32] ibid., p. 17

[33] *The Fellowship of the King* p. 87

[34] Jean-François Steiner *Treblinka* translated from the French by Helen Weaver; preface by Simone de Beauvoir (Simon & Shuster, New York 1967; Weidenfeld & Nicolson, London 1967)

[35] ibid., p. 155

[36] ibid., p. 158

[37] ibid., p. 137

[38] ibid., p. 159

[39] 'The Right to Hope', op. cit., p. 17

CHAPTER 2

[1] Ernst Benz *Evolution and Christian Hope* pp. 226–7

[2] World Council of Churches *The Church for Others and the Church for the World* (Geneva 1967): Final Report of the Western European Working Group, pp. 14–15

[3] Oscar Cullmann *Christ and Time* translated by Floyd V. Filson (Westminster Press, Philadelphia) revised edition 1964 p. 87

[4] G. Huntston Williams *The Radical Reformation*; Benz *Evolution and Christian Hope, passim*

[5] *Hope in Action passim*

[6] *The Works of President Edwards* (Baines, Leeds 1811), vol. viii; part iii, ch. iv: 'Concerning Efficacious Grace', §48, p. 454; the passage is cited by James Sellers, with helpful commentary, in *Theological Ethics* (Macmillan, New York 1966), p. 43

CHAPTER 3

[1] The bibliography on pp. 141–143 gives some of the other current contributions

to the dialogue on eschatology and a few of the older offerings that still make their impact felt.

[2] Jürgen Moltmann *Theology of Hope* p. 16

[3] see Moltmann, 'Hope and Confidence: A Conversation with Ernst Bloch', *Dialog* vol. vii (Winter 1968), pp. 42-55; 'Hope without Faith: An Eschatological Humanism without God' *Concilium* vol. vi, no. 2 (June 1966); for a European response to Moltmann's general thought on eschatology, see Wolf-Dieter Marsch *et al.*, *Discussion über die Theologie der Hoffnung von Jürgen Moltmann*

[4] *Theology of Hope* p. 145

[5] To put it in the vernacular of another age, 'How ya gonna keep 'em down on the farm, After they've seen Paree?'

[6] as he believes Bloch has done; see Moltmann in the article cited above: *Dialog* vii, 50-3

[7] for example, the criticism of Continental theologians in W.-D. Marsch, op. cit.

[8] For the 'godforsaken' theme, see Moltmann *Theology of Hope* pp. 18-19, 31-2, 84-5, 94, 163-5, 196, 213-15, 223-4, 229, 334; but see also the evidence of another note on occasion: pp. 33-4, 105-6

[9] *Theology of Hope* p. 124. He also takes issue with Buber's 'reversing of the subjects' in the former's thesis: 'The redemption of the world is left to the power of our conversion. God has no wish for any other means of perfecting his creation than by our help. He will not reveal his kingdom until we have laid its foundations' (ibid., p. 124)

[10] The crucifixion receives attention, but not commensurate with its importance.

[11] *Dialog* vii, 49

[12] quoted by Christopher F. Mooney s.j. in *Teilhard de Chardin and the Mystery of Christ* p. 16

[13] *The Phenomenon of Man* p. 320

[14] *Le Milieu Divin* pp. 150-1

[15] *The Phenomenon of Man* p. 254

[16] In order to pack as much background material as possible into the text for clarifying the lines of a developing point of view, we shall not use any quotations

[17] For an effort to distinguish these strands, see Gabriel Fackre, 'Secularization: Meaning, Value, Style' *Foundations* vol. x, no. 4 (October-December 1967), pp. 354-69

[18] *Prisoner for God: Letters and Papers from Prison* edited by Eberhard Bethge, translated by Reginald Fuller (Macmillan, New York 1961), p. 159; English edition: *Letters and Papers from Prison* (Collins: Fontana Books, London 1959), p. 118

[19] For a more recent and chastened observation on the persistence of the evil with which a theology of hope must come to terms, see Harvey Cox, 'Radical Hope and Empirical Probability' *Christianity and Crisis* vol. xxviii, no. 8 (13 May 1968), pp. 97-8. The comments of Cox and others in a symposium on 'Christian Realism' are a valuable source for examining the relation of the developing theology of hope to the problem of evil; see 'Christian Realism: A Symposium' *Christianity and Crisis* vol. xxviii, no. 14 (August 1968), pp. 176-90

[20] Harvey Cox, 'The Death of God and the Future of Theology', in Martin Marty

and Dean Peerman (edd.) *New Theology* no. 4 (Macmillan, New York 1967), p. 251
[21] Ct. Gabriel Fackre *Humiliation and Celebration* (Sheed and Ward, New York 1969)
[22] ibid., p. 252

CHAPTER 4

[1] for example, Robert Spike *The Freedom Revolution and the Churches* (Association Press, New York 1965)
[2] 'Needed: A Human Reformation' *The Lutheran* vol. v, no. 23 (8 November 1967), p. 15
[3] Daniel Cohn-Bendit's word for the 'leaders' of a leaderless revolution, underscored in a BBC 1 television interview with a cross-section of the spokesmen of the 1968 protest.
[4] Portions of the following are taken from the article, 'Faith and the Science–Man Questions' *Christianity and Crisis* vol. xxvii, no. 23 (8 January 1968), pp. 315–18
[5] see the remarks of José Delgado in *Human Values and Advancing Technology* pp. 68–92
[6] *Nihilism* translated by John Doberstein (Harper & Bros, New York 1961; Routledge & Kegan Paul, London 1962), p. 91; see also the discussion of the technician in Max Lerner *America as a Civilization* (Simon & Shuster, New York 1957; Jonathan Cape, London 1958), pp. 235–8
[7] Donald Michael, 'Twenty-First Century Institutions' *Human Values and Advancing Technology* pp. 103f.
[8] For a more extended discussion of the polarization and counter-tendencies, see the author's 'The Crisis of the Congregation: A Debate', in *Voluntary Associations* edited by D. B. Robertson (John Knox Press, Richmond, Va. 1966) and 'Princeton Meeting on Renewal' *The Christian Century* vol. lxxxiii, no. 36 (7 September 1966), pp. 1095–8. One of the significant institutional efforts to overcome polarization is the United Church of Christ 1968–69 Emphasis; see *The Local Church in God's Mission* (United Church of Christ, Philadelphia 1968; revied edition)
[9] 'Revolution', by Edith Lovejoy Pierce, *The Christian Century* vol. lxxxv, no. 22 (29 May 1968), p. 712.

Index

acedia, 82, 102, 105, 108
Altizer, T. J. J., 65
Augustine, St., 107

Barth, K., 4, 71
Bell, D., 24 f, 29
Benz, E., 47, 57, 90
Berdyaev, N., 25
black power, 19
Bloch, E., 57, 71, 81, 100, 104, 109
Bonhoeffer, D., 106, 114
Brunner, E., 4
Bulletin of Atomic Scientists, 131
Bultmann, R., 4, 71

Calhoun, D., 4
Canonical Variations, 27 f
Christian Century, The, 2
Christogenesis, 87 f
Clark, Sheriff, 21
Cosmogenesis, 85 ff
Commission on the Year 2000, 24, 29
Cox, H., 2, 3, 70, 97–116

death, 32, 46, 80–2, 87
de Beauvoir, S., 32, 41
Delgado, J., 127
Dewart, L., 100, 104, 109
diakonia, 103
disciplina arcani, 68
Dobrée, B., 24
Docetism, 56

Ebionism, 56, 62
ecclesiology, 79, 95, 137
Edwards, J., 61
Eller, V., 2
Ents, 32
eschaton, 73, 74, 77
Evanston Assembly, 3
existentialism, 4
existential impulse, 99

Feuerbach, 51
Final Vision, The, 49 f
freedom fighters, 19, 41, 127
Freedom Movement, 20
Freedom Revolution, 121 ff

Frodo, 30–4
futurology, 2, 24–30, 62, 98
future-orientation, 9, 11, 17, 28, 33, 42,
    48, 70, 81, 83, 91, 102, 110, 113 f

Gamgee, Sam, 32–4
Gandalf, 33
Ghandi, 22

Haldane, J. B. S., 24
Hamilton, W., 109
Harkness, G., 4
Hauer, W., 9
Heim, K., 4
Hobbit, the, 31–35, 42
Hoekendijk, 4
Hudson Institute, 25, 27
Huxley, J. S., 24

Irenaeus, St., 64

Jews, 21, 36–41, 47, 102 f

Kahn, H., 24–30
Kerygma, 96, 103, 137
Kierkegaard, S., 107
King, Martin Luther, 5, 18–24, 42, 45,
    62, 122
Koinonia, 103
Kraemer, H., 4

Legolas, 34
Lord of the Rings, 32

Margull, H., 57
Marxists, 3, 71, 81, 101, 104, 124 f
metanoia, 132
Menniger, K., 2
Merry, 32, 34
methodology, 25, 28
Minear, P. S., 4
Mississippi, march, 19
    state, 20, 22
Moltmann, J., 3, 70–82, 90, 93, 97, 98,
    106, 116
Montanists, 57
Mordor, 31, 34

Nazis, 9, 36–40, 130
Negroes, 18–23
Newbigin, L., 4
Niebuhr, R., 4, 63, 106, 130
Niles, D. T., 4
Novak, M., 122

Peguy, C., 2
Pelagians, -ism, 61, 62, 77, 93
Penultimate Vision, the, 51 f
Pippin, 32, 34

Secularization, 5 ff, 59 ff, 98
Schlink, 4
Schweitzer, A., 4
Shalom, 50, 52 ff, 58, 61–4, 66, 72, 77,
    93, 96, 100, 103, 105, 108, 118–28,
    132 f
Shirley, Sir Robert, 44
Sorokin, 25
Standard World, 27 f
Staunton Harold, 44

Steiner, J-F., 36
Soteriology, 79

Teilhard de Chardin, P., 4, 33, 70, 84–
    97, 100, 104, 107, 116
The Year 2,000, 24
Thielicke, H., 131
think-tanks, 25, 27
Tillich, P., 4, 30, 43
Tolkein, J. R. R., 31–35
totalitarian movements, 9
Toynbee, A. J., 25
Treblinka, 36–42, 111, 118, 126
Treebeard, 32, 34

Visser 't Hooft, W. A., 4

Weiner, A. J., 24 ff
Wells, H. G., 24
Williams, G., 57
Willingen Conference, 4
Wilson, McNair, 24
World Council of Churches, 61, 100